The Doorway to Nature

Books by

Raymond T. Fuller

WALK, LOOK AND LISTEN
Sign Posts on a Naturalist's Highways

THE DOORWAY TO NATURE

ALONG THE BROOK

The DOORWAY *to* NATURE

by Raymond T. Fuller

The John Day Company

New York

About the Author

RAYMOND TIFFT FULLER was born July 23, 1889, in Syracuse, New York, and lived in northern Oswego County, New York, as a child. The love and intimate knowledge that he has of outdoor life goes back to the time of his boyhood there.

He studied at the Biological Laboratory at Cold Spring Harbor, New York, and at Colgate University. After being graduated from Colgate he taught for several years in High Schools and Progressive Schools, and in Washington and Jefferson College. He then traveled in Australia and the Orient as representative for a chemical company, and has since made many trips around the world.

Mr. Fuller is the author of WALK, LOOK & LISTEN, and ALONG THE BROOK, and has contributed articles to the *Nation, Century, Travel, Mentor, Good Housekeeping, Better Homes & Gardens, S. E. Post, North American Review,* and many other magazines.

"You Come Too!"

"Just come outside and I'll show you!"—this I overheard one belligerent individual shout to another in a city restaurant not long ago. It then struck me that this phrase would make a good title for a stack of manuscript upon which I was working—although too long. What *could* such a man have shown his companion outside—except perhaps a few stars!—for the two of them would still have been *in the city?* Now, if they were to come out into the country . . .

I prefaced a former book * with the remark that a sort of patriotism for my own countryside had caused me to write it; had urged me to show strangers around—even as a bigger-and-better-town enthusiast "points with pride" to his community's high-spots. The present volume (once the above-mentioned stack of manuscript) is another outcome of the same irrepressible fervor.

"I'm going out to clean the pasture spring;
I'll only stop to rake the leaves away
(And wait to watch the water clear, I may);
I shan't be gone long. You come too.

* *Walk, Look and Listen!* The John Day Co., New York, 1929.

The Doorway to Nature

> "I'm going out to fetch the little calf
> That's standing by the mother. It's so young,
> It totters when she licks it with her tongue.
> I shan't be gone long. You come too."
>
> —ROBERT FROST.

Suppose you are one of those who "don't know anything about Nature"; once you did not know how to read books or even how to walk. Your children are glad you learned. Children in this city age have a right and a need to learn nature-lore, too. And who are better comrades in the process than their parents? I cannot help quoting the words of a famous professor of biology. He once said to me: "Whenever I wanted to learn a new branch of the natural sciences, I offered a course in it!" By studying it with his students, he taught himself best of all!

Contents

Contents

Part One
OVERCOMING OUR SHYNESS

How Shall We Start?

I BELIEVE that if a census could be taken of wishes —such a one, for instance, as the Department of Agriculture is taking of fishes—a certain longing would be discovered in the heart of the Average American Parent. The longing is this: "I wish I knew *something about nature*—how to take along the kids and really *see* things! Owls, 'possums, cricket frogs, luna moths, woodcocks, wild ginger . . . the outdoor things Burroughs wrote about."

A naturalist going about lecturing starts up that sigh as commonly as he flushes rabbits out of October meadows. Scores of parents, he finds, are not satisfied with merely *reading about* nature adventures: they want to *have* them!—And, bless them, why shouldn't they become "nature-minded," along with becoming "air-minded" and "two-car-conscious"?

Average American parents are busy: sixty-two per cent of them are city-dwellers. In the very nature of things, how shall they go about it to gratify that desire?

Here's a suggestion. But wait! Before I offer it, I must make a plain, blunt statement, man-

to-man. Wherever the city, the town, the neighborhood, in which you live, you have no valid excuse because of its location for putting off a first-
hand acquaintance with Nature. Your automobile
brings your home as near a sufficiently wild section as you need ask. It is astonishing how small
is the diameter of a city's cankering influence; how
close to town wild roots grow and wood folk
creep! Draw an hour's circle (40-mile) around
Boston's City Hall, Manhattan's Columbus Circle,
Philadelphia's Broad Street, Chicago's Loop,
Pittsburgh's Downtown; and you enclose areas
comparatively rich with wild life. I know, for I've
been in all of them!

But why not start with your own backyard?
Around a suburban dooryard are more things than
meet the eye—at first acquaintance. A little further
on are plenty of suggestions that may aid you to
discover what you little realized was so close at
hand. That little pest who tunnels your lawn, for
instance; the creature which you may have thought
was merely a Mole turns out to be the Mole Shrew
(Blarina). A family of Red Squirrels, whose adults
are early risers and infinitely sly around their true
home, may actually be tenanting one of your bird
houses. (How they love meat scraps or a bone to
nibble, thus to slake somewhat their unholy pas-

sion for baby birds and eggs!) Two, or even three,
species of salamanders may have for years hidden
under your decaying boards or rocks or in stumps:
they are fascinating indoors in your vivarium, in
spite of being mainly nocturnal. In early morning
or just as the summer daylight fails, an occasional
half-hour spent in nosing inquisitively about in
odd nooks on your grounds often yields the ela-
tion and thrills of discovery.

Odd moments, as well as odd hours, slip by
while you spend time indoors reading or puttering
at some inconsequential task. Springs and summers
are so short; precious days slip by so quickly;
what with rainy intervals or dull gray hours inter-
rupting; that before one realizes, the opportunity
for certain nature experiences is past and gone
for yet another year. . . . I must make here a
strong point.

If you are going into this nature game—*budget
your time.* One is sure to live beyond his income
if he does not budget living expenses; and if one
does not likewise budget the time to be given to
the kids and nature-study, he will let invaluable
days slip away never to be retrieved. Oh, I know
how it is! Baseball games, gardening jobs, golf,
interfere. Business trips come up, callers drop in,
football Saturdays crowd into the autumn. Pres-

ently and unawares, another year has gone by; you are a year older and no nearer that hoped-for intimacy. It becomes a question of *values*, of *choices*. If you are seriously after the illusive acquaintanceship, pick out such week-end dates as these—and adhere to them!

Mid-April: For hunting frog-eggs. For ten earliest spring flowers. For locating a Screech Owl's nest. For letting spring in general sweep through you to far better effect than the treacle-and-molasses treatment of our forefathers.

End-April: For trout fishing. For repeating all of the above. For listening to the famous "evening hymn" of the Woodcock, and the winnowing of the migrating Wilson Snipe.

May 10th: When Azalea is in bloom, and Dogwood. When infant Crows are hatching, and the woods are full of Jack-in-the-pulpits, and the last summer birds are arriving. Now is the week when the Brown Thrasher sings, and one can bathe, glass-in-hand, in the northward "wave of warblers" going through upper United States.

There is middle July when they have cut the hay. How *different* all the meadows seem after haying! There's so much activity in the butterfly and insect world in August: set down two dates for August! There's aster time in September. There are thirty days in November when you can go hunting co-coons, watching squirrels get ready for winter, counting the Bob White and Grouse families which are still flocking together after the murderous hunting season. And so on. But budget your days—and keep the appointments!

Let us have it out with the automobile! A blessing to those far from the country; the nature-lover's boon. It can take you to it, but it cannot go with you into nature-land itself. Be under no illusions. Perhaps one *can* see mountains, rivers, prairies and oceans from a motor car; but he cannot possibly learn to know nature. As the old adage has it: You cannot run until you can *walk*. No royal road to nature—above all, no concrete highway. One cannot serve two masters. Gasoline and nature mix no more than oil and brook-water. For millenniums human eyes have been geared to the speed of human feet. This is a basic psychological fact: the brain absolutely cannot take adequate note of surroundings at a pace faster than a walk; it will not form images that *remain* as memories. One can no more see and remember the outdoor world from an auto than he can take snapshots from the Empire State Express.

Certain preferences are sure to come very early in the belated effort towards familiarity with nature. The trend will be very definitely toward one or perhaps two phases of nature. It may be birds or insects or aquaria or botany—whatever it is the home should be connected with the hobby. No naturalist worthy of the designation ever left his hobby outside the doorstep. Even the big-game hunter (if he be a naturalist and not an un-naturalist!) will bring back heads and horns. However out-of-doors the pursuit may be, it will have repercussions at home. Indeed, one may be judged as to his actual and real interest by the evidences showing in his housekeeping.

For a series of nature experiments full of exceeding interest, I can recommend the following to any family. These contraptions bring nature into intimate observation and are sure-fire means of arousing in the youngsters a hearty appetite for further adventures afield:

(1) The Observation Beehive.

(2) The Indoor Ant-hill.

(3) Self-stocked Aquariums.

(4) Vivariums for the Salamanders, Frogs and small Snakes you may happen upon.

(5) Cages for Chipmunks, Squirrels, Hares, Chucks, which you can trap in the neighborhood by home-made box traps.

(6) Plants, as insect-breeding cages, using

flower pots holding the proper kind of plant for the species bred, and covering the plant with an inverted lamp or lantern globe topped by a square of screening. (In such little transparent cages many insects will go through all or part of their life histories right before your eyes.)

Full directions for making and operating these are to be had from books which your librarian or book dealer will dig out for you.

Now for the suggestion. . . . Buy a big rectangular aquarium—but don't buy anything to put into it. Go out and get your own tenants. Take a quart jar and a handled kitchen-sieve, or a larger, stronger, wider-meshed utensil such as is used to lower doughnuts in deep fat, about ten inches across its bowl and flat-bottomed. Get into the car with Bob and Jane. Drive to a reasonably rural brook and start prospecting. You will in no time have captured so many water creatures that it will take several succeeding evenings' home-work to get them all named. Under stones, in the mud, on weed-stems, hiding among debris on the bottom —you, in your old clothes and regardless of wet and muddy feet, will have the time of your life seeing things, finding things. How will you know whether you have captured Asellus, Caddice,

Hellgramite, Damsel Fly larva, Hyla, Crayfish, Daphnia, or Salamander? Well, probably you won't until you have spent hours over the books your librarian hands out to you. After which you are sure to discover that you have several other brook dwellers besides.

Now, to keep your fishless aquarium running true to nature, you will have to read up on the whole subject of aquariums. But this can readily be done by anyone who will gamble on the chance that the more he finds out about anything, the more fun it becomes.

If your mind happens to run to the liliputian and you possess a good magnifying glass, you will find among the debris of your aquarium such tiny things as Hydras, Daphnia, Cyclops and Cypris. Here is an interesting thing to do. Get a dozen test tubes and a rack. Set them at eye-level before a window. In each tube you can segregate and breed different minutiæ like these. Watch their activities, their life cycles—as important in the scheme of things as yours and mine—be introduced thereby to the ever-concentric wonder which nature spreads all about us. The only apparatus: test tubes, city water and a medicine dropper. The initiative to start?—ah, there's the hardest part in all this "back to nature" business!

Equip yourself with a self-starter—the rest follows.

While we are on a watery subject, let me suggest another beginners' project. Set out in April and collect frog eggs! Hardly a quiet ditch or small pond in the woods but will yield egg-masses of one or more varieties. Look for semitransparent, cloudy handsful of gelatine dotted with black specks. Likely you will have to do some ankle- or knee-deep wading—be prepared for that. More than likely when you start for home laden with four or five full quart jars, you will have certain salamander eggs and three varieties of frog eggs. If your expedition is later in the spring, you may have toad eggs, too. When you get home, put a shelf across a window, face-high, and on it arrange a set of jar aquariums. Place in each what appear to be different species or stages of your egg-masses. Now let Nature take her course. Get *The Frog Book* from the library or bookstore; and your nature-yearning mind will never be quite the same again!

June is the at-home month of the birds. If you wish to learn a few birds, devote your June weekends to it. An old orchard or a neglected upland pasture are two ideal places. Take two things— and do two things: opera glasses and a bird-guide;

keep still and keep at it! One bird leads to another. Once you have learned a dozen you are
fairly launched and it comes easier; a process of
elimination of the known helps you to focus more
intelligently upon the unknowns in the bird-guide.

In sober garments, sit half-concealed and use
your magic glasses to transport you clear around
the vicinity. And for locating nests—or rather, for
allowing the builders to locate them for you—no
technique is so successful as this sort of watchful
waiting. Other grist comes to the mill of the quiet
watcher: a fox sneaks past; a weasel slips winding
along from nowhere and disappears into the same
place; Gray Squirrels and Red take their children
out for lessons in gymnastics and bread-winning.
Once a Shrew tunneled right under me as I sat
looking for birds, and I succeeded in bringing him
out squeaking into the daylight to exhibit his truly
shrewish traits while I gripped the nap of his neck.

After having read a book of mine an until-then
unknown friend wrote:

> You may be interested to know how I took my first
> tottering steps in Nature's nursery. . . . Went every
> Saturday to a different spot in those woods, and just sat
> down and *looked*. Every plant, every tree, every insect
> and bird I did not know the name of, I made notes on
> as I sat. Plants I took home to identify. To my amaze-

ment, in one spring I had learned more of nature than in twenty-five whole summers before.

This idea is worth passing on. To make such a census as that demands a conscience and a holy determination. *Everything in sight!* A rigorous measure, but in this case, at least, successful.

If one's interest turns out to be insects, he is in particular luck. He will, for instance, be able to keep bees. If at home he has an out-door area ten feet square, he *will* keep bees. And, of course, if he but has a window facing the sun, he can put an observation hive against the inside sill of that window, and so set the entrance that the bees go and come through the slightly raised sash. An observation hive is one cunningly enclosed in glass, over which sliding sides are fixed. By sliding back a side, the entire secret life of the hive is bared. Both real honey and real nature-lore are dispensed by such a hive, which can be bought at any large bee-supply house.

In addition to bees, your "beginner in bugs" may build himself an observation ant-hill. The fascination of the educational movie (or even, indeed, of the mis-educational kind) has nothing on such home movies as the hive and the hill. Directions for constructing an indoor ant-hill are available in at least five books which I have. Your librarian, reflecting your own interest in just about the intensity you flash it upon her, will dig out the books whose names I need not mention here.

If you go on from these conquests of bee and ant, there is a whole laboratory for insect breeding to be had in a dozen or fifteen potted plants. A miniature insectary can be made by putting lantern-globes around the plants to serve as transparent cages. All this technique is set forth by master entomologists in their books.

As one of the first of your nature sallies, go "cocooning." Between November 1st and May 1st take long walks in thickety, bushy places, looking for moth cocoons. Some years my own family has collected ten different varieties. After you have learned in a general way what to look for, you are likely to make a success of this cocooning. Take your finds home for the winter; keep them in a non-heated room, a screened porch—even a screened box will do. The dryness of heated houses kills the dormant larva inside the silken raincoat. When they emerge at odd times all through the following spring, especially if you have been lucky enough to watch the strange process of resurrection itself, you will get what the children call "an awful kick" out of cocooning. Then detain your emerged moth—if it be a fe-

male—inside a screened box, window or porch, in
order that she serve as a lure to all the males in
your end of the township. Where perhaps you
never had seen a Luna or a Cecropia all your days,
that ineffable odor the moth wafts into the night
will infallibly bring from two to two dozen suitors
of her species. An intriguing sport, this cocooning,
and often with unlooked-for sequels.

The time to make your initial start in learning a
few hundred wild flowers is, of course, in early
spring. There's hardly an early wood's plant
which will not stand transplanting into your own
garden spots, even if moved during this early blossoming period. The ten earliest spring flowers in
the eastern states above Mason-Dixon's Line are:
Skunk Cabbage, Hepatica or Liverwort, Adder's
Tongue or Dog-tooth Violet, Arbutus, Trillium,
Dutchman's Breeches, Bloodroot, Wood Anemone, Saxifrage, and Spring Beauty (Claytonia).
If on every walk, you bring home at least five
new blossoms and learn their names with the aid
of a standard flower-guide or two, by the end of
your second spring, you will awake one morning
aware that you are in a fair way to become a botanist. I don't wonder the uninitiated but wishful
quail when they face the whole vast list of our
native plants. To know even a fraction appears a

stupendous task. Then, those two or three hundred technical botanic terms—which apparently one must master before he can even begin identifying from the books—how formidable a catalogue it is! Yet be of good cheer. I who have travelled the road from the Dandelion to Hooker's Orchis, assure you it is not so hard. Not hard? Nay, it is joy itself.

I consider that conquering one's antipathy toward—I will not call it fear of—snakes, toads, spiders, caterpillars, and the like, is a most important start toward becoming familiar with nature. Until you can see real beauty and enduring interest in such traditionally spurned creatures, you are not likely to make your nature quest a success. Both beauty and interest are there. Steel yourself, fight yourself, if necessary, to pick up the next harmless and friendly garter snake you happen upon. Handle toads and frogs every time you get a chance—it's the first time or two only which count! Children do not "inherit" such fears from parents—they *imitate* them! If the children have already imitated some "daring" and uninhibited teacher or companion so that everything that wriggles, squirms, hops, or oozes, is to them merely one more interesting thrill and not a shudder, then the shame of the reluctant parent should be deep. If, on the other hand, they have such in-grained reluctances, great will be your reward in casting out their squeamishness. One of the most memorable hours of my life was spent persuading a group of twelve children that snakes *really could be handled*. The process was not carried out by argument but by example. All were inwardly squeamish at first, but none would reveal it to the others; and presently all were successfully pretending that they had handled reptiles from baby-hood.

One of the difficulties every old hand encounters in taking children into the wilderness to show them things, is to keep them quiet. Yet it is absolutely useless to attempt to study Nature unless one is as still as possible. Notice how the country boy, who has learned to hunt, fish and follow his dog from childhood, walks through the woods. Notice how riotously his city brethren do it. The first will encounter and see ten times as much. . . . But children are not the only folk who unconsciously regard a country walk as a conversational event. Shake off such adult "companionship" and go alone—the smaller the party the larger the game.

One day last June I chanced upon three of my friends who had just come through the same piece of woods I had. Our converging paths brought us to a roadside spot at the same moment. I had found the nests of a Northern Water-thrush, a Towhee, a Chestnut-sided Warbler; had seen a 'Possum asleep in a crotch, watched a Fox still-hunting for mice, collected four Cecropia cocoons, flushed a litter of twelve Grouse chicks, counted five Gray Squirrels; and I forget now what else besides. Yet my friends had had such a good time discussing Debussy and Reval that they now offered the opinion that these woods "were getting all hunted out." Music and philosophy are grand subjects for talk—but absolutely not in the woods. There let the leaves do the talking!

It goes almost without saying that even if you school yourself to quietness in the woods; if you carry a high-class pair of binoculars; if you keep eyes and ears at their openest; nevertheless, it will be the *number of times* you indulge your outdoor desires that will give you the adventures and encounters you crave—and make you a companion and stimulus to your children. Even one summer vacation in truly backwoods country, spent largely in the daily pursuit of outdoor experiences, will thoroughly initiate the most complete tyro. Keeping everlastingly at it is a sure recipe for putting the zest in nature-stew.

Just Outside the Door

"NONE so blind as they who will not see!"—so runs the old adage. This saying, however, applies to points of argument and reason. When it comes to actual eyesight the phrasing had better be: "None so blind as they who *cannot* see." At least, that is the way a naturalist would put it.

Not that faulty vision is to blame. Even good eyes have their "blind spots." As I have noticed, there are two reasons why the average city and near-city person does not observe the half that out-door creatures are doing under his very nose. One is that he doesn't care to poke about and watch a little; the other is that he doesn't know just what he ought to be looking out for. Perhaps, also, there is yet another reason; he doesn't at all realize what a lot is to be seen in the way of nature exhibits, even at his very doorstep.

This knack of being observant seems usually to be discussed as if it were an inborn gift, and that some of us have it and others simply do not. Now, as a matter of fact, I believe you will agree that nearly every one of us is observant. Some, however, note certain things, others very different things. For example, certain of my friends awe me completely by the minuteness with which they take in and remember just what "the new styles" are. They can tell you almost to a thread what someone they met was wearing, and that, the day after the meeting. Another sort of acquaintance will be able to report after an automobile ride which make of car is most popular on the road. An architect who comes to visit me will be picking out superb sites for a country home where I have only seen Rabbit's-foot Clover and Painted Cup growing, or some equally inconsequential (to him) bit of nature-lore. Thoreau once answered a companion on a walk, who asked him how one went about finding Indian arrowheads, "Why, your mind must be stored with arrowheads." Which was his peculiar way of stating that one has to know what to be looking for; what to have stored in the mind's eye. Well, that is what I mean. Once you come to realize what an astonishing number of interesting creatures are stealthily carrying-on around you; even in places you have come to think of as thoroughly "spoiled" from a wilderness point of view; and have acquired a hint as to how to go quietly and slyly yourself, there is a lot to be found.

The other night about dusk, while I sat watching a pair of Gray Foxes playing around on the ledges in the field next my home, it occurred to me that if I treated my own home record as a sort of case history, it might serve as an incentive to others and something "to shoot at." Getting others interested in observing nature is an evangelical weakness of mine. When it became too dark to see the foxes any more, I went inside and got out my nature diary. What follows is gleaned therefrom. You are welcome to check-up on it any time you are in this vicinity.

We do not live away back in the country—if we did there would not be much point in setting down these paragraphs. On the contrary, this present domicile is much too near a large city to be all that a nature-hobbyist desires. A high-powered rifle, shot from the back porch, could send a bullet across two busy motor highways; and I can see, in the wintertime at least, twenty-five neighboring houses. True, there is a fine piece of woods adjoining which may serve as a "feeder" for the more immediate stock of wild life. But this is regularly strewn every week-end with newspapers and lunch-box debris, and is supposed to be thoroughly domesticated by the process. So much so, indeed, that acquaintances of mine refuse to use it as a nature-seeking ground, but will, in spite of my remonstrances, motor away off into the next county in order to revel in no more than I do right here. However, my reveling has to be done before nine A.M. and after six P.M., and during weeks when the motor picnicking urge does not send its quota of newspaper readers out this way. Three acres and a brook, bits of thicket and a joyful number of trees, comprise the range and cover of the place itself.

To start with, an eight-year record has yielded a list of ninety-two birds which have been seen on and from these boundaries. Naturally, few technically called "water birds" appear on the list, such as ducks, geese, gulls, plovers and herons; although not a few have been seen going over on migrations or passing up along the little brook in late summer. At random, I pick out a few species in order to give the drift of the bird-life hereabout. Woodcocks are not uncommon: one pair— and I am certain it is the same pair—has been with us all the year round ever since I can remember. Every March, along about the 10th, the male starts his daily courting antics at sunset, and gives us a thrill at each public reappearance. Although supposed to be a courting or mating exhibition, its skylark flights and song go on nightly for six or seven weeks; long after the irresistibly appealing little chicks are hatched in the near-by thicket. Thereafter, their presence is ascertained by tracks in the mud along the brook and by frequent flushing of the birds from various daytime coverts. Black-crowned Night Herons, coming over to their nests in the treetops of the woods, are seen almost every evening. Here are a few others: White-eyed Vireo, Yellow-throated Vireo, Northern Waterthrush, Cardinal (a pair stayed one whole March here), Sharp-shinned, Red-shouldered, Red-tailed, Cooper, Marsh and Sparrow Hawks, Veery, Chat, Orchard Oriole, Green Heron and Mourning Dove. Besides these and the commoner residents, an unusual number of migrants passing through swell the total. Nearly all the latter, with very few exceptions, have been observed during one season or another. As for both resident and nonresident members of the warbler clan, the most notable are: Worm-eating, Blue-winged Yellow, Canadian, Hooded (found breeding), Black-poll, Kentucky, Bay-breasted and Blackburnian. According to U. S. Biological Survey investigations, the country as a whole supports a trifle over one pair of birds per acre. Here, however, we regularly have ten pairs nesting at once, on three acres.

The little Brown Rabbit is our commonest mammal. What they and our last year's family of Woodchucks have done and can do to garden and flower-beds, need not be discussed here. Vegetarians must live, the same as other creatures. For the past three summers a female bunny, for whose extraordinary tameness we have no explanation, has performed her racial duties so earnestly that the place has become quite a rendezvous for rabbits. The recent advent of an Airedale has lowered its popularity somewhat, although a delectable two-pound youngster is—as I write this—taking advantage of the dog's absence and is enjoying some fallen apples. Why he should be, at his age, too, so surpassingly shy and elusive, being the off-spring of a thoroughly trusting mother, is a matter for conjecture. Possibly he got the shock of his life when I took him and three brothers from a nest under a tussock on the brook bank last May and kept him penned during his most impression-able period. This makes the third litter of young actually discovered in nests on these demesnes. The woodchucks, father, mother and whelps, had to be driven away by persistent persecution, so ruthless did they become in the garden during dry spells. The maternal chuck developed a notable canniness before the summer was over. Her den, being so open to surveillance, was no place for her to loiter about, so she often decamped early and stayed away all day. Occasionally I would see her sneaking back from a long distance, and have watched her perform the trick of running along the stones and shallows of the stream to get far away into the next lot. Finally, I hit upon the idea of erecting a white cloth scarecrow in front of her den. That evening I saw her return to it. On catching sight of the object—hardly larger than herself—she distinctly started as if she had seen a ghost. It was some minutes before she passed it and entered. From that night forth I never laid eyes on her again!

Both the Star-nosed and Common Mole are resident here, but not commonly seen. A Short-tailed Shrew, whose den is probably close behind it, makes an under-mud runway down to the water after every freshet which has swept the former one away. Deer and Red Foxes are infrequent transients; Raccoon tracks I have also noted in winter snows. Red, Gray and Flying Squirrels are, like sensible small fry, more often heard than seen. Despite the fact that city hunters with pump-guns and rifles crowd the neighboring woods in the autumn, shooting down anything that moves, our two Gray Squirrel families do not seem to diminish annually. They are holding their own, but at the expense of foregoing the daylight after eight in the morning. By full and proper use of beds placed close alongside chamber windows, early morning observation of both animals and birds has been greatly increased; and bird and squirrel nesting-boxes have padded our census. An occasional 'Possum wanders over this way in the autumn; one I caught in my hands in the road. I boarded him for a few weeks. (Rather, I should have said "her," for she had the marsupial pocket for small-change on her underside—although, at the time, she was out of funds.) How she did enjoy raisins and apple cores! A Red Bat or two frequents our blinds during his northern stay, and somewhere on the place is a hollow, yet undiscovered, which must be sleeping quarters for a few more. They are not hard to catch in the former nook, and our whole family feel well up on bats and their traits. About the time the last of the four Chimney Swifts turn in for the night down the flue, the bats spell them for the never-ending warfare on insects.

It would take up too great space here to say much about insect life on the premises. Insects are everywhere in any event; and there are always more varieties than one can attach names to. On summer nights, keeping female moths (using females of the showy Giant Silkworm family) in our screened-in porch as lures has given us some of our keenest thrills. The record number of males lured to any one mate was fourteen. Our count was all-too accurate, for it was made from the number of pairs of wings lying on the ground next morning. Either screech owls, bats, or nighthawks did this grisly job, shearing off fat bodies from wings as fast as newcomers appeared. We never knew which ogre it was. . . . Diligent search for moth cocoons each autumn, after the leaves are off, has sufficed to supply us with a spring crop of resurrecting beauties, and to build up a magnificent collection of them for one of the children.

Although the stream furnishes as interesting a natural aquarium as is necessary, it is a little hard to control such a lengthy one. Therefore, in the house we run from one to six artificial pools of glass, and always bring up from the egg an unconscionable number of hyla, frog, and salamander fry every April. We have learned how much is added to the attraction of an aquarium, large or small, by shelving it against a window.

We have kept an apiary of several hives outdoors, having also had the happy experience of maintaining a glass-backed observation hive inside a window.

Needless to say, we have a garden. In selecting flowers, special attention is given to such as will attract butterflies, moths and birds. Hummers like the tube-throated varieties: nasturtium, trumpet vine and gladiola. Butterfly bush attracts its namesakes. Cosmos, milkweed, sunflower and other of the composite family are delights to the goldfinches and migrant seed-eaters. We have compiled a list of wild flowers here; this year the total of sixty-three varieties was reached, omitting shrubs and trees.

But the most alluring feature of all in the cultivation of nature study at home is the constant and steady occurrence of *new things* to see. Something exciting is always turning up—like those gray foxes over yonder. Now, one would never suspect they were there, within twenty rods of a concrete road and a house. And who would have imagined a skunk taking up abode underneath the henhouse, and never touching a feather or an egg all through one autumn? The long drought this summer caused a six-day migration of a large colony of the red-and-black ant; the endless amount of experimenting which we could carry on was the feature of the whole season. A foot-wide stream of them, transporting their black slaves, their pupæ and larvæ, flowed on across the lawn for over three hundred feet. We never could follow it to the new nest, so dense was the grass and thicket at the further side. For those who cannot readily go to wilder localities as often as they wish, their intensive attention to all the nooks of the home grounds and its neighborhood will yield about as much of marvel and surprise as they have time for, along with all the busyness of life today. . . . Aristotle's dictum—"Know thyself!" may be paraphrased for them into: Naturalist, know thine own backyard!

Before Eight A.M.

DISTURBING as it may be for those to whom nature-lore is a delight, I humbly proffer the opinion that there are millions of Americans who never see a summer sunrise for years together. I have already met a number of them first-hand. Not that it is, in the first place, any of my business; not that there is any moral virtue in getting up occasionally before dawn; and not that there is any outstanding thrill or loveliness in a sunrise *per se*, which cannot be gained from a sunset; I merely state a fact of perennial interest to me.

It is apparent that city and town living has done for sunrises what it has for the moon, the stars and the weather—simply taken such things completely out of the observation and ken of the vast majority. Of course, the immediate threat or promise of the day's weather, as it affects daily affairs, still holds some concern for them; and sometimes they get brief glimpses of the waxing moon or catch a fleeting sight of a colorful sunset. Certainly we all enjoy warm, hate hot, cringe at zero days. But as for anything approaching our forefathers' interest

in the daily features of the cosmos—no, not nowadays; no matter how much the full moon figures
in our popular songs; or the nightingale, or the
whip-poor-will, or the great, wide-open spaces.
. . . And, that, I think, is rather too bad.

Especially, when you realize that but yesterday
the human race's whole culture hung upon natural
phenomena, today's indifference to them is quite
remarkable. Nature provided man with his divin-
ities. Sun, moon, planets, stars, mountains, ocean,
yielded gods to him. His early religions came directly from nature. From the same source we had
our calendars and clocks; we celebrated holidays
marked out by the Earth-Mother. Weather for
crops, soil fertility, water supply, grazing conditions, sailing, fishing, the changing seasons, were
all matters of universal import and concern. Indeed, so vastly important was the weather; so
deeply did it impress itself upon our consciousness; that today we are constantly making conversation out of it as if it really mattered. But to most
of us, it doesn't at all.

We have become city folks—sixty-two per cent
of us, at least, dwell in city or town. Everyone has
a watch, a wall calendar, a food and water supply
at his elbow, a time-table and a motor car. Apparently, then, amid swift traffic, tall buildings, close

dwellings, tree-lined streets and cliff-side apartment houses, there is very little to draw our attention to the everyday things of nature. We go so fast in automobiles that, wishful as we may be, we can catch but fleeting impressions of the world above and about. Our visual perceptions are not yet geared to the speed of a car.

The foregoing being commonplace to us all, what is there of moment to say about "Before Eight A.M."? Well, it is exactly *because* of this state of affairs that a nature-lover wishes to introduce urban and suburban Americans to what, in large measure, they may be quite unaware of: the astonishing number of nature experiences to be enjoyed in early morning. How can they know what dawn-rising is like if they never try it? Neighbor Stiglitz often repeats that "before eight A.M. is the best part of the day."—That's what suggested the title of this chapter.

Few city workers leave home before that hour. If they did not prefer staying up late at night, what a lot of zest they could get out of an occasional before-breakfast excursion. Did I say *to the country?* I did not. Even in a city park, or in the neglected spots at the end of a street in Suburbia, there is something to discover, and more to watch. That is, if you care for that sort of thing. If you don't now; if your attempts at it awaken no spark; there's your children! Children I have known almost invariably show an enthusiasm for outdoor life if given a chance. We parents can help them, and ought to. At any rate, there it lies, this yet unobliterated field of interest, perhaps unnoticed, right at your very door. Once you develop an eye and a taste for it, this early morning nature-walk is one of the most invigorating common interests a family ever tried to share. The children cannot join in your evening diversions—it is only fair to bring them in on something before the absentee work-day starts in the morning.

Sunrise. . . . You are up and out. Perhaps in the sky itself there is no greater beauty in sun-up than in sun-down: evening's progressive light effects are reversed; the same long slanting shadows come that somehow make landscape more alluring than full day. But dawn is something besides mere sunrise. First, there is a different zest in yourself. You are fresh and rested. So are the outdoor creatures. Birds actually put more life into their songs at dawn than at evening: it has often been remarked. The air is bracing, cool. There is always a lot more going on among outdoor creatures. In practically all localities which people frequent after the day's work begins, the birds and animals are forced to do most of their foraging before human beings are stirring. Only too well have they learned our sleeping habits. Crows will reside all year round and build nests in scant woods remarkably close to houses; but may rarely be heard or seen while the sun is high. Before it is light they will slide up to the garbage pails and the chicken-yard or explore the brook bed back of your home. You will often startle them away by the first window you shut or door you open. Squirrels, both red and gray, do their collecting of maple and ash keys, apples and unripe nuts, in your dooryard trees long before the family is up. Where perhaps their very existence goes unsuspected for weeks, squirrels (and chipmunks) will be living around among your shrubbery and that of your neighbors. Only when you awaken earlier than usual and lie gazing outdoors will you catch sight of them.

Sunrise. . . . The Screech Owls are just settling themselves for a day's nap in the leafy tangles. Rabbits are out in the open feeding. They invariably hide after the dew is gone. I have seen five on my lawn at one time. This spring in my three acres, a quarter-mile from a concrete highway, I found two litters of six babies each, snugly nestling in their fur-lined nooks under grass tussocks. Watching the mothers at dawn led me to both finds. The Blue Jays rove fearlessly around at dawn; Woodchucks get so assured that human enemies will lie abed another two hours that they carelessly range many hundred yards from their burrows. Many other creatures, shy and retiring at noon-day, act at sunrise as if they had learned they would be little disturbed.

Right here I insert a suggestion. I would urge everyone whose rooms look out on anything more than walls or roofs, to put their beds at the windows. I don't understand just why it is, but in nine-tenths of the homes you visit you find the beds in the room corner or along the side opposite the window. If you will place them so that when you awake your head is where you can look out over the surrounding trees, lawns and bushes, you will be likely to observe a surprising number of happenings in nature. That you will also be able to admire clouds and sky, and discover a new time to drink in to the full the loveliness of the flowers and grounds on which you have spent so much time, need hardly be said. Few of us get time enough during daylight to enjoy with leisure the charms we have created about us. For the summer months, at least, sleep with your head at the window!

If you are watching there—say on the mornings

you do not rise early and take your walk—you may see where the Humming Bird or Song Sparrow or Robin is slyly building its nest. Right under your nose birds will sometimes make a nest which escapes your notice. Many of them do this work early in the morning exclusively; and most of them labor busiest at the job then. Dawn is unquestionably the time for bird study.

Dew is over everything when you start. You must expect damp feet and ankles unless you protect them. Those who know dew only at night or just before it disappears in the morning, can have no idea how glittering and glistening a thing it is under the horizontal rays of a rising sun. A little higher climbs the sun—and the jeweled reflections are gone. Dew literally "gilds the lily"; it is Nature's polish, making second-hand things new. Study under a magnifying glass a dew-soaked spiderweb hung at right angles to the rays. So amazingly do its threads resemble strung pearls, you can hardly believe your eyes. Pick and eat your wild blackberries and strawberries with the dew on them if you want flavor!

The supreme serenity of water is never impressed upon you more than at dawn. A lake, a pond, or even a small marsh pool, is transfigured. Above it, perhaps a suspicion of mist cloaking the farther bank; on its surface, it wears the sun-shot, dew-washed mornings as if each were the Primal Morn itself; Creation's day, newly stamped, freshly pressed as if just emerging from the mint where worlds are coined!

It would be worth while to walk like this at daybreak if only that the familiar sounds of human activity are absent. Only Nature makes herself heard. An inescapable feeling of unreality can come over one at this hour. Half unconsciously one walks in another world, an elder world into which all this complex busyness of living has not yet come. To ancient man, Nature was a companion; by modern man, she is looked upon as a casual stranger.

Man has gone far in his contempt for Nature. He has tried to level her forests everywhere and to subjugate all soils to his planting. Fire of his setting has ravaged countless acres; his herds roam the prairies and his plow changes the face of them. Wild creatures he would exterminate wherever he sets his dwelling. He has made oceans serve his purposes, and through the air and across the hills he has driven as though they were his alone. From his cities he has exiled every thing primeval save weather—and except in storms weather stays above the housetops. He has made night into day, winter into summer. He has balked drought by irrigation. His manifesto is that he will not be content until he has made all the earth pay him tribute.

And yet, whoever has attended upon sunrises has been made aware somehow that in them at least there yet resides an ancient spirit untouched, untamed. Man has never been able to conquer the dawn. The day is his, and the night also, but dawn is still a sort of covenant between earth and the cosmos. . . . Man has been only too successful in his campaign against Nature, so that, where his victory has been most complete, only at sunrise do her green pennants and the voices of her stragglers proclaim an eternal resurgence and an unbaffled intention.

Dawn is but a legend to most people, for they rarely or never see it. Yet it is possible that we would lose some of our jaunty assurance if we looked oftener upon the sunrise and realized that Nature, far from being conquered, is every day quietly asserting claim and patiently watching to advance wherever we relax vigilance. A naturalist notes how the world of timid creatures ignores or forgets the daytime dominion of man. There is a period of perhaps two hours after sunrise when even at the walls of our busiest cities, you will find birds and animals and insects who manage to act naturally and unafraid. The weeds in our garden, the pests at our fruit, mock our sense of complete dominion over the earth. The morning dew, the mist along the brook, the frost, the earliest breeze —all these come and go at a 1930 sunrise as they did in 1630. Sunrise can gild the stark walls of apartment houses and drab lines of identical city dwellings quite as though such were not in fact the tents of its enemies; and it can lie shimmering upon factory roofs and mill windows as though caressing its own. There is strangeness in such forgiveness of the foe; such blessing of the enemy's colors—if, indeed, it be not sheer and indifferent contempt.

"See a sunrise every week!" I commend as one of the slogans of every nature-inclined citizen. To do so, at first, takes real initiative, but imparts a glow of Spartan heroism. There is no use in trying to put this resolve into effect unless one is willing to curtail his night enjoyments. One cannot serve two masters: midnight and daybreak. If you start out to walk, you may damage the first few trips somewhat until you arrive at the realization that you must travel with the sun at your back. Never walk directly toward the sun if you can avoid it; all you will see is silhouettes.

Take your binoculars or field glasses; compile that list of 100 birds. Take the butterfly net; help your boy and girl make their collection. Take a dredge net and a pail; add a dozen odd denizens to your "fishless aquarium"; bring home frog eggs in the spring, and tadpoles. Arrange another aquarium for brook fish only. See if you can stock your vivarium with the dozen species of salamanders to be found in the East. Go in for a snake den; there are seven common varieties which are harmless to handle but educative to watch. Set out some traps for catching chipmunks or squirrels alive, and make true pets of them. Increase your garden flowers with a score of wild natives easy to transplant and tame. Ferns, too, for the shady nooks. Indian relics, minerals, fossils. Find ant colonies to stock your homemade ant-hill. Learn to identify every forest tree in your range. Census a brook from end to end. Do any one of a dozen things like these—with your children and for them. The first thing you know, you will find yourself entangled in some hobby or other and you'll never be quite the same again—Before Eight A.M.

I don't suppose golf can be played without clubs

and balls, or tennis without courts and rackets.
Country club memberships cost money; so does
bridge. Baseball involves an outfit and a field;
sailing, a boat and accessories; auto-camping, a lot
of impedimenta. Every hobby or pastime or exercise nowadays requires certain investments in
gear. So why should not nature-study for families
mean buying some contraptions and apparatus? It
should, and must, if you are going to get much
enduring fun out of it. Why not let yourself go a
little on this nature business: aquariums, cages,
field glasses, collecting nets, guidebooks, window-
boxes, observation beehives, vivariums, insect
mounts, magnifying glasses, etc. Much of the paraphernalia you can make, and that's a good thing
in itself. In any event, it doesn't total up much
expense in the end, but (like bridge) there is no
foreseeing a limit to the hobby itself!

Daylight saving is undoubtedly the single greatest step towards the enchantment of *living* for the
city man since the Saturday half-holiday was in-
stituted. The next important move is just around
the corner: the five-day working week. That is
almost upon us. But the reason why the present
writer urges stretching the day in the opposite direction is not because it is healthy, wealthy and
wise, but because he has found, from thirty years

of experience, that for nature-lovers the first two hours of daylight is worth all the rest of them together. It is not so much leisure that we need as it is leisure before breakfast! Ask any old time trout fisherman.

Auto-camping on Nature's Trail

No doubt but that for the majority of us today, the path back to nature cannot be begun on foot, which is the right and ancient way, but will start at the home garage, lead out along the concrete; and end at some place we like where things grow without benefit of fertilizer.

One who yearns to become intimate with nature will follow this itinerary for the sole purpose of transport (as has been intimated a few pages back), ruthlessly parking when he gets out of sight of habitations; and from then on using his own sparkplug of enthusiasm for operating his own biped mechanism. Why walk, in this motor age? somebody will arise and ask. Why, bless you! walking—because now profanely called, hiking—is the very antidote our biological system needs to offset the effects of modern noise and haste. Ask your doctor, if you have one, whether you are wise to hitch laziness and speed together and call the combination "progress." Sweat is a veritable elixir of life. Actually, we *must* use our large muscles for health. If we are too bound down to a house or a salary to pursue some active sport, walking is the perfect substitute. It is as good for the sole of the foot as for the crown of the head. But all that aside, a nature hobby *must be* a foot hobby.

The "motor age" phrase is a pretty euphemism; an economic expression only. For the era of oil stops short at the green edge of "the age of insects"; an epoch in which, the scientists maintain, we human mammals now exist. Two hundred yards from a farmer's line fence, the things of instinct are oblivious of man's cleverness in transportation. To them, the motor age is an incident. Naturalists see that Man is the only creation of protoplasm that regards travel as an end in itself. . . . In sixty minutes at the most, from any home in America, we can reach a spot practically unaffected by automobile traffic.

Auto-camping. . . . It transfuses gypsy blood back into our veins. Astride a steering wheel, we re-create ourselves into a hybrid of red Indian, nomad Bedouin, covered-wagoner and twentieth-century scientist. We preserve the best features of each and escape the hardships of all. Magic carpet, Aladdin's ring, Cinderella's pumpkin, Bellerophon's Pegasus! We are our own Lewis & Clark Expedition. Or, alas, we are only motorists!

I believe that I state a little-realized fact in

saying that very few autoists camp. By themselves, I mean. You may drive during daylight along a route so crowded as to render the trip a stupid, nerve-racking procession; the roadside so ugly and belittered by an unesthetic mob that it turns you sick under the diaphragm; and yet, at nightfall, turn off up a quiet dirt road for a half-mile and locate a delectable spot by a jingling brook. You will usually find no evidence whatever that anyone has ever spent a night there before! Compared to the thousands of folk who pass along a highway in a day, the number stopping for sleep in a secluded nook of their own choosing is as a fraction of one per cent. . . . It has been an astonishing discovery! The itinerant nature-lover is rarely at loss for an undisturbed place to pause a day or so. I have proved this on a score of long trips. Either autoists do not at all understand the simple technique of the thing; or they do not "dare" to spend the night out; or the proceeding has no appeal whatever to them.

Pass one of those abominations to the venturesome spirit, a public camp site or a roadside tourist corral, along toward supper time, and you will likely see it jammed to capacity with cars and paraphernalia of every description. (Such tenement-house sojourning is actually known by the name of auto-camping in some vocabularies.) Yet go your way past to a near-paradise by a brookside, amid birds, bees, woodchucks and flowers; and ten to one, you will be Adam's original family in an Eden where no apple has been plucked. Incredible, yet a fact. It is even more incredible, and equally veritable, that those who own the legal right to the spot rarely say no to your request. On your part, give them no cause to regret it! No scrap of paper left behind, or other rubbish. Your use of firewood and your care for embers should leave no bitterness to those who own the land or to those who come there after you.

You may know these piecemeal Edens, oasised throughout a sinful world, by two tokens. One is a lane or bit of terrain over which to drive so that your car and tent are hidden from the by-road. The other is a bit of level land at the other end whereon to pitch your canvas. Further features are not so essential. (I have on occasion ridden with people who were trying to find such a spot for the night, to whom it simply did not occur to stop the car at various places and go on foot to investigate. But this practice is almost always necessary. A few moments' walk down a lane or over a hill will locate many a likely site. It is partly because few motor addicts will deign to do such a thing, even when they wish to camp, that these hundreds of untouched sites exist.)

One must be adaptable to the demands of all secondary features at the place chosen. Not even drinking- or cooking-water need be at hand, for you may bring a night's supply from some well you have passed on the road. Modern machine production sees to nearly all the rest. The tent you buy, the utensils, bedding, foods, are all so cunningly fashioned to your needs that if you do not possess, and for a small expense, what every legitimate comfort demands, it is your own innocent fault.

But, I hasten to insert, to carry a camp outfitter's store complete, to bring along scores of so-called accessories made mainly for catchpenny purposes, is inept and costly. It cramps your style and balks your ingenuity; it ties you to the city with a cable-tow. To insulate yourself by an armor of contraptions and to intrench behind a breastwork of city-made devices designed to defy Nature at every point, will of course, defeat the purpose of your trip. Nature retreats in spirit before you as she is attacked with these weapons of offense. Somehow, simplicity is the keynote to put you in tune with The Song of Songs which is

Nature's. And that is a secret worth knowing.

Assume that you have found the by-road, the land, the site. Perhaps haying is just over; the meadows shaven and shorn. Good sites are now multiplied. How attractive almost any old orchard is at this time! You covet such a spot: easy to drive beneath the trees and over the knolls out of sight. If it borders a little creek, your cup drips over. . . . At this point, if you want it, I put down a brief list of essential equipment to unload from your car, a list resulting from the experiences of a family of four over many a delightful excursion: *

Tent, umbrella type, 7 x 7. (Solve the very important question of mosquito-control before you start out!)

Two blankets each. Some folks demand folding cots. We don't. We enjoy sleeping on the ground-cloth of the tent above one heavy blanket. Tiny pillows usually go along, too.

Shovel. For making a ditch around the tent to turn off heavy rains.

Small axe. Although we never find much use for it.

Heavy grate, with folding legs that push into the ground. This makes cooking much easier, especially when rain compels one to cook beneath the tent door, used as marquee.

* A good book on auto-camping, full of details and useful hints, although some of its information is now out of date, is *Motor Camping* by J. C. and J. D. Long, Dodd, Mead & Co., 1923.

Fry pan, skillet, pail (for coffee, mainly), *water pail, two canteens, an army mess-kit apiece,* complete the outfit for cooking.

A very short list, this! A few minor accessories are not mentioned. Traveling from place to place in a car, neither your tenting nor food problems are of very meticulous concern—as they would be for hikers. I do repeat, however, that plenty of fine bobbinet against mosquitoes is worth more than its weight in platinum; and if you are out in "punkie" (or "no-see-um") seasons (June-July mainly), cheesecloth screening is imperative. These latter pests work at night, and on some occasions only a good smoke-screen smudge will keep them wholly out.

Near habitations beware of drinking stream water until it is boiled, although I feel that this sort of danger is greatly overstressed. It appears from personal observation that the majority of Americans are so accustomed to buying everything they eat that they commonly never think of adding wild strawberries, blackberries, huckleberries and edible fungi to their menus. Yet each, in its season, is a common and widely distributed delicacy. Every year, near my home, I am able to pick quarts of high-class blackberries around the fringe of a roadside picnicking and camping site, for no one else seems to have noticed them.

Learning to Walk

I AM quite sure that even the most taciturn of us will at times discover we can hold forth at great length—if only someone gets us started on our favorite hobby. Before a sympathetic (or possibly long-suffering) friend, we are surprised to notice that our habitual incoherence and shyness disappear like summer dew. We find ourselves running on and on—and, oddly enough, really saying something!

After Neighbor Stiglitz left the other day I bolted into the house and jotted down most of the conversation which I had found so pleasant, only to discover that it wasn't a conversation at all; it was a monologue. Neighbor Stiglitz has that effect on me. Only a few weeks ago we (or was it I?) got going on so fatuous a pair of topics as the idiosyncrasies of Guinea Fowls and the wonders of their concrete-shelled eggs; and before the pipe smoke cleared away, we had put in a whole hour —and no garden planted! (But that's another story.)

It was Walking this time. He couldn't have speared me in a tenderer or more vital spot.

"To walk successfully (I heard myself saying), one needs to be familiar enough with trees, flowers, animals, birds, insects, stones and crops, to call them by their first names. Also, one needs to know weather, farms, cities, books, and people."

"Walking, then, has little to do with legs and feet?" he queried.

"Little. I believe a person has to learn to walk, just as he does to swim, or to keep books, or to buy stocks and bonds. Not every let-loose city denizen—or bound-to-the-land countryman, for that matter,—can make an occasional excursion on foot in the country, and get much more than a languid two per cent dividend out of the investment of his time."

"Is it a difficult art to learn?" (Stiglitz is the sort of fellow who gets out his car if he has to run down to the corner for a tin of tobacco.)

"Not at all. Only it takes a little time. But it's somewhat difficult to *want* to learn." I was warming to my work. "That's where the pinch comes. The vicious circle lies in that until he learns a few steps, he cannot understand how much fun it is. To *want to learn* how to become a walker is likely to develop into a jeopardizing menace to a city man's business. Your busy, tied-down individual would get all stirred up, have his attention distracted and be uneasy much of the time, if he went wholeheartedly into walking as a hobby. Returning to 'normalcy' would be no easy matter. For tramping, as you will agree, Stiglitz, is a cultural accomplishment, an athlete's task, a writer's safeguard, a philosopher's pastime, a poet's necessity. Whoever heard of a prosperous man of affairs being all these, and yet prosperous?"

"There you go, being intolerant again!" interrupted my listener. "Aren't you a mite hard on the person who has other interests, perhaps, and just as broad a zest in other lines?"

"Not so hard on him as he is on himself; for he does not know what he is missing. Excuse me, neighbor, for using the pronoun 'he' all the while. I think I must have given up the women of the country as fellow walkers about the time my wife discovered that it was practically impossible for her to buy a pair of flat-heeled shoes anywhere. Astounding fact! She didn't want golf or tennis footwear; she craved mere comfort. So utterly have nonpedestrian shoes become the choice of American women, that only a few concerns make shoes for feet any more—they make them for motor cars. As universally as have *men* become

addicted to automobile riding, they still *can* walk
a mile if necessary other than on a floor or a side-
walk. But women . . ."

"You nature cranks hate the auto, don't you?
You are so old-fashioned."

"Utterly wrong, Stiglitz! You know perfectly
well that I own a car. It enables me to enjoy many
more contacts with the out-of-doors and to do actually a greater amount of walking—because it
can *take me there*. It cannot go with me *into*
nature-land, but it puts me at the entrance—at a
dozen entrances where I couldn't have gone without it. No, we hiking enthusiasts know our gasoline—we can take it or leave it alone. We have
put the motor car in its proper place."

"Amen!" said Stiglitz, a little dubiously, I
thought. Then he asked: "What kind of an outfit
do you recommend to us beginners?"

"Outfit be hanged! That's the least of it. Outfit
sort of gathers around you as you go on making
wider and wider circles of adventure. But since
you ask a natural question, I can make some suggestions. First, footwear well-broken-in and sufficiently oversize to enclose two pairs of socks; inner
cotton, outer wool. Not calf-high walking boots—
Heaven forbid! I've never felt the need of them.
They're heavy, hot, stiff, and often settle into a

wrinkle or two behind the Achilles tendon which excruciate you. . . . Old clothes, the older the better. An extra sweater. A German-style rucksack for your shoulders. A shirt with a pair of breast-pockets. Water canteen—when you must carry water. Binoculars—the little but powerful kind— for they enlarge your whole scope immensely, and are absolutely essential if you are bird-minded. Your cooking utensils should be aluminum, sim-ple, and few: A one-quart boiling pail or pot, a cup, a tiny fry-pan and dish combination such as the standard army set, with its knife, fork and spoon. Carry a stout pocket-knife as well. A change of socks and underwear, a pair of sneakers for eve-ning wear. A set of U. S. Geological Survey maps covering your area, mounted on cloth. Your six-pound walker's tent to carry rolled on top of the rucksack—no pegs, no pole, for those you cut at night with your knife."

"No hatchet?"

"No hatchet. . . . Two light wool blankets, a waterproof poncho, mainly to walk under if it rains—or to sleep on when pitching the tent is not necessary. A couple of yards of bobbinet to defeat mosquitos is almost an essential. And that's all."

"Don't you have to eat?"

"Stupid of me! Your food is to be largely

chosen by weight. In general, the more a food-stuff weighs *per cubic inch*, the more nourishment. You must depend mainly on concentrated provender, unwise as that is for the regular home diet. Oat- and corn-meal, a whole-wheat loaf, bacon, powdered milk, sugar, soluble coffee or tea, bouillon cubes, chocolate, raisins, triscuit, dates, peanut butter in a jar, rice, sardines, dried beef, dried soups—the imported kinds are best, hard-boiled eggs, and such as that. Don't leave salt and and pepper behind. The very minimum of toilet requisites and a towel, I neglected to mention a moment ago. Only experience can list the knick-knacks that add weight but, also, some satisfaction.

"When would you advise going? I'm getting excited!"

"When the spirit moves you—any time between April and October. As I hinted before, the walking-lust is deucedly inconvenient. The urge to drop all and follow the winds is apt to come to people at stated periods. There are, for instance, ten times a year when some of us must willy-nilly get afield: a walker's Red Letter—I should say, Green Letter—days. Annually he looks forward to these ten, and when each of them arrives he rejoices. . . . What did you say?"

"Only 'go on.' "

"According to the Gregorian Calendar, these are movable events; but not so in the schedule of the seasons compiled and arranged by Nature's almanackers. In that elastic natural calendar, to which man's is but a rough and general guide, what corresponds to months depends on the weather: not upon the sun, as do man's. Some years, for example, Nature's March runs past mid-April, and October holds well up into December.

"Earliest comes Woodchuck Day. (No, not Candlemas Day, at all!) The walker is abroad in the crusty, noon-melting snow of late February. He has been shut up and buried by winter, just as the ground has. . . . He sees, with an annual thrill, afar off on the white expanse a small slowly-moving object. As he nears, the object resolves itself into a thin uncertain Woodchuck, now sitting with drowsy wits abruptly keyed to watchfulness, beside his burrow. Even with snow over all, the animal has not forgotten the exact location of his summer dead-line around the hole; and, as if it were wired with an electric burglar alarm, the moment it is crossed by you, the chuck automatically disappears. Coming to the spot, the walker sees the white surface tracked about by mud from below. He regards the event as of great augury, for some peculiar inkling of contingent spring has reached the hibernating marmot deep under the frost, signaled along by wireless through the ground. Soon the whole countryside will get the news!

"A full moon often attends the week of Wood-chuck Day: true walkers will go out o' nights. The Skunks have begun to come from their short hiber-nation—you may follow them from henhouse to den; the Great-horned Owls have begun hooting throatily o' nights—you may seek their nests; Foxes are getting desperate for food; Raccoons for corn from the crib, Squirrels for the nut caches deep under the snow, you stand a better chance of seeing them all just now. At what other time of the year can one travel the woods by night? Stealthily, tirelessly, as an Alaskan Indian, one now makes the annual tour of inspection even to the last and loneliest acre of his range. Hard crusts to bear his weight; wide white expanses; the sleeping forest; the nipping and eager air!— It is drop bread-winning, and go!

"Then, to all northeastern ears, what is of more moment than the first Robin arrived in March?— bringing with him 'the morning's mail of the sea-son,' as Thoreau said. Spring begins for walkers with that premier Robin, though it may be May before spring enters the towns. (But, of course, no overnight hikes for six weeks yet.)

"Hardly has this Red Letter been recorded than another is upon us: Hyla Night comes with the thaws when retreating winter is hastily destroying his munitions of ice and snow, soaking them with pelting rain, washing them away by freshets, covering his retreat with fog screens and curtains of mist. It is a night full of silvery pipings, calling one to steal outside and let the cool humid breeze blow his hair as he drinks in the molten sound. Of this Hyla sound, the listener breathes: 'The air hath bubbles as the water hath, and these are of them.'

"Then comes the spring slowly up this way. The fourth whisper is sent. Plowing time, orchard blooming, the month of birds and flowers, trout and young leaves. You *cannot* let this period go by without a dozen walks! A busy, stay-at-home interval follows, which lasts until about mid-July.

"Now sounds the most imperious ukase of all! Haying is finished. The year has turned a corner; henceforth to saunter down hill from the heights of expectancy. Something in the clean-cut meadows on bottoms and upland suggests an alien country, a virgin land calling for exploration. For months we have looked to satiation on the neigh-

boring countryside, seeing it grow grass, daisies,
buttercups, tall weeds; seen fields over which
wind-ripples roll and shadows float; and we have
got used to it. Then, the mowing machine. . . .
Of a sudden, overnight, a new land surrounds us:
moors, downs, heaths, untrodden highlands. Rich
meadows are transformed into stretching pasture
and strange prairies. Walking now is easy for the
feet, nothing moving can escape the eye. We must
be off!

"Hot days, summer droughts intervene. Drow-
siness, dryness settles over nature. Bird songs
cease, for it is molting time. Weeks run on until
August broods above the finished corn—summer
at flood tide. Then, one hot day bursts that annual
storm. Winds that shift into the north. After
hours of drenching gusts—it is no longer summer.
An electric vigor upsets us: the first auroral fore-
taste of autumn. Walks lengthen into weeks and
fortnights. Mosquitos have gone or dwindled into
insignificance. We walk and camp, and camp and
walk, until we are for the time satisfied.

"The first frost renews our ardor. This marks
the eighth disturbance in ordered living. Many
dates in Nature's calendar hinge upon that first
frost: nuts are warned that they have to split up
their hoardings with the rodent clan; woodchucks

begin to carry in dry stuff for a winter bed; foliage gets its notice; witch-hazel starts blossoming; the earth's green hair starts turning brown; for that white warning is an earnest of what is coming. IS it a graphic warning to those birds which migrate, a sort of wall-poster for the illiterate? Come, set your house in order, it says to life, against the north wind's keen inspection! The Fringed Gentian is the trophy most sought; when we find the first one, we cut another notch in our walking-stick.

"The ninth upset is caused by the . . ."

"I know what you are going to say next: 'The earliest snowfall.' " I had almost forgot he was there!

"Right, Stiglitz, the snow. And lastly, the time of mid-winter snow, when it is deepest and lightest everywhere. Even those who pretend to like living in the city become affected by it. Some call their urge 'winter sports,' but at bottom it's the same compelling unrest that worries us out here in the country. Thereafter, one can settle himself with complacency beside his fireplace at moments when his work relents, without a constant compunction that he should really be outdoors lest he miss something. For him, Nature's fiscal year has closed."

"Always you speak of 'the countryside.' Don't you ever go anywhere but around this immediate vicinity? Me, I feel I have seen it all."

"Stiglitz," I said impressively, "do you feign not to know that there is a mountain system called the Appalachians extending from Georgia to Maine? Have you yourself ignored the White Mountains, the Green Mountains, the Adirondacks and the Catskills, the Ramapos, Kittatinies and Alleghenies? Well, I haven't. And there is no reason why you should. You own a fairly respectable six-cylinder internal-combustion traveling conveyance, and you pay *some* income-tax, at least. Go ye into all the hills and spread the gospel of walking!"

After considerable pause during which he was apparently searching for words—whether to justify his leglessness, or to express his conversion, I could not make out—he moved toward the gate. *"C'est le premier pas qui coute*—I see it plainly," he murmured.

He had uttered a pregnant remark, although in a non-American tongue: It *is* "the first step which counts!"

Here ended our conversation. But since I have set down so much already about how to walk, look and listen, I may as well add here a certain program of Nature Fêtes, which, so far as I know, is not printed and distributed to the public at large. It is of great value to walkers and those learning the art. These fêtes form a series of "exhibits in exterior decoration" which demonstrate what one artist can do in a year, if you let her work and give her plenty of time.

Doubtless through imitating his surroundings, man caught his trick and habit of decorating in celebration of events that interest him. Considering his resources he sometimes does rather well. But Nature is the original celebrant, the master-decorator; her stores are boundless, inexhaustible. Nature has her festivals no less than man. She decks her green communities in eastern America on at least a dozen occasions during the year. And on an open-handed, state-wide scale, too; it is not done by halves.

Around May 1st occurs the "Fortnight-of-the-spring-grass" fête, during which red maples, elms and poplars are employed with dainty and exquisite effect above the greening carpet. A little later appears Lilac Week, so dear to the heart of native New Englanders. The air becomes heavy with one of the world's richest scents. A tour along country roads finds every homestead hung with

purple. Such holiday-weeks come crowding at this
season: the next event being Dogwood Days. Con-
currently, forming the domestic feature of these
days, peach and cherry, apple and plum, reach
bloom. But no wild blossoming yields deeper delight than the Dogwood's. The tree's buds before,
and the red fruit long afterward—even the twigs
in winter—are particularly satisfying.

Hardly is this week gone than the Laurel Pag-
eant floods the pastures and open woods in an en-
chanting flood of pink-and-whiteness. As at the
stroke of a wand, an amount of sheer loveliness
leaps from the unwarning valleys, which every
year seems incredible, even to an expectant native.
Rhododendron takes up the laurel motif wherever
sufficient elevation permits it, and adds during its
brief celebration, a tropical touch to the woods, an
effect that the daintier laurel misses. If we pass
over the less dramatic events of Blackberry Flowering (which, somehow, few notice!), Tulip-tree
Week, and the period when the wild grapes send
forth strata upon strata of perfumed air along the
highways; we would next notice the occasion by
which summer is formally inducted into office:
Daisy Time. If you have not seen the meadows,
already lush with buttercup and clover, take upon
themselves, of a sudden, broad sheets of damask

daisies; you have no idea of the lavishness of the process. Innumerable daisies carry all before them, from now on until haying puts ruthless stop to their invasion. One week, not a flower has opened; the next, as far as you can see, daisies.

Autumn's inauguration is planned by Nature with a similar sweep. Joe-Pye Weed vies with Purple Aster and ubiquitous Goldenrod to make a most sumptuous setting. Virginia Creeper leaves trace scarlet arabesques across the gray of stone walls; Poison Ivy smothers them in orange bunting. . . . At last, the decorations of the year culminate in that high-tide of coloration: Autumn Foliage. In certain years for a week—rarely more than that—the leafage is most gorgeous: miss those few days, and the supreme touch of splendor is lost.

Usually I prefer to take my walking "straight," undiluted by conversation, particularly when I wish to stalk or study wild life. Traveling with a donkey may have suited Stevenson; but you never can tell how asinine an otherwise gifted person will turn out when you tramp with him. Good conversationalists, like writers, have their own peculiar hours and surroundings during which they can create best:—some, it appears, when sharing a day's hike. But it seems to me that talking is a nocturnal art, to be practiced before hearths, at clubs, or in easy chairs. In woods and fields talk is wholly out of place. We go there to escape talk, not to make it. Walk, Look and Listen—I defy you to do all three, and *talk*, too!"

Do not imagine that all these paragraphs are intended as the defense of a Lost Cause, nor as an elegy for the Walker That Was. Just as too many motorists spoil the roads, too many walkers will clutter the trails. Something evanescent vanishes when a beautiful thing is charged by crowds. This is not a carping at democracy; I merely point out an inherent quality in nature. Cities are for crowds; the wilderness for escaping them. No cause for misgivings, however. We who walk will be few . . . But there are nowhere near enough of us!

Spring-in-the-Fall

TODAY the calendar contended it was autumn. Impudent sheet! September 30th, indeed! Trying to curry favor with me, weren't you, shrinking old pad, reminding me today is a birthday!—Fawning, paper-souled thing that you are!

The door banged behind me. I started out across the garden toward the woods. In the dewy sunshine symphony which the morning was playing recurred the very motif of spring. Allegretto. Alfresco. . . . Spring-in-the-Fall.

Just as I reached the stone wall back of the orchard, I had to meet Bob bringing the morning milk pail. Bare-foot, whistling, open-eyed, he came. He was spring, too! "Many happy returns, Mr. Fuller!" he shouted.

Confound the lovely lad! Suppose I *was* forty-five—what of it? A man is only as old as . . . Bosh! I *was* Autumn—why not face it?—To-day *was* Fall—why not accept it?

I sat on the wall to think about it. Four months ago it was May. Thirty years ago I was Bob. Trite reflection. Not much comfort in that! . . . At my

second blooming. Spring-in-the-Fall. Yes, there
was such a thing. Good way to put it. Be thankful
for it! Some solace in that. . . . "Backward, turn
backward, O Time in thy flight; make me a boy
again just for . . ." While I sat there, at least,
Time *did*. . . .

I changed my mind about going for a walk in
the woods: a man on a birthday may do as he likes.
I would loaf. . . .

At ten I did not know these things: that the Boy
is but the Man writ large, that the Boy is Father
to the Man. At forty-five here on the stone wall,
I was a man of substance, safely home. Inside and
out I was monarch of all I surveyed. I had a Full
Covenant Warranty Deed to the view. But, somehow, a monarch like Lear, whose empire was a
stormy heath. Over life, after all, I had won a
Pyrrhic victory. . . . Bob, now.—There is a
king for you!

Bare-foot, whistling, open-eyed, the Boy Monarch: what he surveys he is lord of. Unaware. In-
cognito.

While he reigns over it, blissfully for him, he is
forbidden to know that the state "Happiness" is
sierra, not plateau; a range, not a mesa; that it has
deep valleys between its peaks. Like a certain King
Louis, he *is* that state. A perennial conspiracy of

the Elders tells him—and he believes!—that a boy walks the *foot* of that mountain road which climbs to the topmost castle; that the years alone will guide him to those sublime battlements above on the tablelands of blue. An unconsciously jealous conspiracy. Envy is back of it—but we call it Wisdom. . . . If he but knew he were ruler there already, gazing without surmise down into the sunset! Did *you*—then?

Away with this conspiracy—I'll none of it! I resign, I flout the cabal!

Emerson flouted it, too. Always hitching wagons to stars, always honest, he gave as his prayer for all humanity that theirs be the attitude of hungry boys, demanding of the world only food, shelter, and to be let alone. . . . And most of us Lears, in secret moments, agree that youth is the chief compensation for the struggle of existence: those days when we bowed neither knee nor back, nor realized that life expected us to.

Compensation. In the first fourth of our lives we drink at the springs of illusion, gorge at the table of dreams. We are tended and groomed. We tilt the chin of Fate and laugh into her omnipotent eyes. During the remainder, we are required to pay off the promissory notes we carelessly signed to pay for all this. Life becomes a debt of honor.

It is only natural that we resent balancing the account. Though some settle like sportsmen—and become respected citizens; others openly protest—we call them poets or hoboes.

But—I call on Freud as witness—even where the world suspects it least, there slumber uneasily throughout adulthood the dreams of what the Boy-left-behind most wanted to do at the moment he was called to account. Entangled in a job, the suddenly-made man lays aside the purposes of his youth; hoping from day to day, then from year to year, to go on with the plans he has dropped. Let him but retire on a competence; let him by some chance be toppled from the squirrel-wheel he has been whirling; and, as he dusts himself off his thoughts turn back to that time when life caged him. He will, of course, rationalize or disguise his desires; he will dress them in garments to avert the neighbors' ridicule; but think them inwardly he will—whether to "save his face" or his life. All along he has subconsciously deemed himself the hunter, engineer, farmer, baseball pitcher, inventor, he once meant to be. Now, if Opportunity slyly renews her offer at fifty, he merely resumes where he left off—so he imagines.

In the times ere the barons of factory and counting-house had wrested from him his Magna

Charta; and his native Bill of Rights had become to him a Bill of Particulars; the Boy Monarch on the New England farm had one regal prerogative devolving upon him, a duty which was a priceless privilege, though he knew not. A task fit for a boy and denied to merchant princelings and heirs expectant of riches: getting the cows up for milking. From *Who's Who* I would like to cull a certain vital statistic: how many in it whom the world's voice is now calling, began by calling the cows? Eighty per cent therein admit beginning life in the country. Few country lads have not served their time fetching the herd to the barns!

It is a June sunrise. Bobolinks are rioting above the dew-soaked meadows; the very air is packed with songs. A father's voice has called from below; the boy sleepily rolls to the side of his bed at the attic window, fumbles for the shirt on the chair, then, stepping into his other garment, he slips the one functioning suspender over shoulder and pads half-awake down the stairs. From the woodshed door he emerges, gathering awareness as he goes. Jack, the collie, bounding from dreamland with that instant energy peculiar to dogs, dances on ahead, acutely nasal to each gossamer stratum of scent.

Past the barns and on across the barnyard, over

the lane bars which he lets down, along the lane,
itself, seamed by the erratic trail cows blaze when
they are bound somewhere. Straight away now to
the pasture woodlot above which the sun is just
lifting. The knee-high corn along the fence at his
left is rustling sleepily to itself; on the right,
lusty potato vines are panicled with white flowers.
The jubilant freshness of dawn seeps into him.
He swings his arms and starts aimlessly whistling
as drowsy robins do—"the earliest pipe of half-
awakened birds." To his hardy soles the close-
cropped grass is stuff of Hamedan; to his uncal-
loused palate wild strawberries are as pomegran-
ates and love-apples. Leaflets of tangy wintergreen
beguile him, too. . . . A distant musical bellow
rings out like a brazen trumpet; away off in the
pasture the cows have heard him coming. Another
throat takes up the call in another key. The
loiterer is reminded of his duty and breaks out
singing "Co' boss, co' boss." Jack, already half a
mile ahead, is shattering the fragile morning by
peremptory barks. The herd is started on its sedate file toward the land, crowding into the barn
at last, each to her own stanchion without guid-
ance. . . . Here dad and the hired-man take up
the ritual. In due-and-ancient form the farm day
is begun.

Another morning that boy will recall. In October. As usual accompaniment of a full moon, the first frost of autumn has crisped and stiffened the night. He shivers as he dashes his face with glaciated water at the pump. The cows are more reluctant now to answer. Toes get numbed. What pleasure to stand a moment on the warm place in the turf where old Betsy has lain all night!—Like burying bare toes in a bearskin rug. Now there are apples to munch, and the daily race with unwieldy woodchucks breakfasting along the fence. A flock of Bob Whites whirrs away as the dog approaches; from the pasture creek now and again of a morning a brace of ducks will airplane flickeringly into the distance.

Of his round-ups for evening milking, the boy will remember best the lengthening shadows of a torrid August day. He sets forth languidly for the pasture, plotting a course from blackberry clump to blackberry clump; and, with the accurate verdict of Jack's nose, investigates potential skunk dens, quasi rabbit burrows and barely possible fox holes in the woods where the cows have filtered feet some wild strawberries had launched into their deeply for its cool shade. Winter trapping will be coming before long—and a hole is a hole for a' that!

The boy who fetches the cows brings with him the whole countryside, and carries it in his heart a whole lifetime to be his solace and his regret.

Did I hear a whistle! Was that Boy starting for his cows? No, it was Bob coming back with his empty milk pail. And—of all things—he was trying to whistle Mendelssohn's "Spring Song"! I waved him out of sight, and glanced down again at the strawberry plants at my feet. They were doing a Spring Song too. They often do.

Nearly every autumn the quiescent plants break forth into bloom again, eager to replenish the earth with a hundred seeds now that the dull duty of weaning their offspring runners has ended. I had picked blossoms every month of the year. Straight through mild winters, stray flowers can be found in sheltered nooks. Clever hot-bedders have so encouraged this emotional tendency that they have produced (from the garden varieties) "everbearing" strains which yield the year around. But cultivate as they will, that subtle essence, that ethereal flavor, horticulturalists cannot wheedle from the secret laboratories of the fields. These qualities never come through a garden gate. Like the bobolink that nests among them, strawberries will not rhapsodize at the tap of man's baton.

There is a poetic justice in that field strawberries cannot become an article of commerce. Not
even are they capitalized to the extent of appearing upon the menus of sumptuous city hotels to
which little else is denied. Like the gold apples
of Attic fable, field strawberries turn ashes when
used for mercenary ends. There is but one place
to eat them: within the square-mile where they
grew. No hireling may be sent for them; save
only him who is to eat thereof. Even as Niagara
cannot be known by proxy, or Hawaii's flowers be
seen through another's eyes; so does nourishment
not come from strawberries picked by merchan-
dizing fingers. Let men who buy and sell keep to
such devitalized fructifications of their gardens for
trafficking, but withhold their hands from the
fields. Only country lad and farm-wife may lay
tribute there. Few among us who have shaken the
pollen-dust of country meadows from off our feet
deserve to eat wild strawberries.

It is not only a failing of strawberries, boys and
retired captains of industry so to lose track of time
that they break forth blossoming all out of tune
with the pitchpipe of May. Nature seems to have
a subconscious as truly as do the thwarted buds of
human society. Many plants exhibit similar lapses
of judgment and perception. Beguiled by honeyed

breezes and a cozening warmth, they yield impul-
sively to the illusions of springlike weathers. It is
as if Nature so loved her spring that she reverts to
it on every opportunity, regardless of what calendars say. How human to be always dreaming
Mays!

Spring-in-the-Fall, a sort of a sixth season, an
interlude before our fifth one, Indian Summer.
Something in it inevitably suggests a spinster's
second blooming, a hoping hopeless pathetic wist-
fulness. It is a sort of Faustian penitence, a barren
wedlock, dowered with memory instead of promise.

American literature is forever singing of autumn's colors—the flaming of reds, yellows,
oranges and umbers. But it overlooks October
blues. First, the unflecked limpidity of the sky on
certain days. Only the stuff from which April
"mends her cloud-veil rifts with blue" is of so rich
a dye. Capri, perhaps, off in the ineffable Bay of
Naples, "pestled by sunshine in a mort of blue,"
knows its like—not as a season, but rather as a
perennial matrix which is too common. But to
stand upon a hilltop during a morning when their
great southward migration is on, watching "the
crows flying high above as they do only on such
days, forms of ebony floating across the azure"

(as Burroughs said), is to experience a new vividness in azure. Also, there is a color, a fringed-gentian-blue, unique to October. And, in some localities, the wild aster in its first flush of unfaded vigor actually drowns the searing fields under floods of cobalt. The lapis lazuli of the ocean off the eastern coasts rises in autumn to its highest market quotation. I have heard old salt-water fishermen ascribe it to "the cleanin' effects o' sunlight," which is perhaps their way of making poetry.

Not alone by blues does autumn recall spring; there is a whole group of happenings which sometimes conspire to produce this transitory sixth season. Bird songs are being learned and tried out by adolescent singers on their first southern trip: White-throat, Fox Sparrow, Winter Wren, Hermit Thrush. Tiny grasshopper nymphs begin hatching from eggs laid too late in summer. Fruit trees, Forsythia and Lilacs start flowering again, and grass around spring-holes and little brooks sometimes has the April lush far into the frost weeks. The big hawks start screaming and circling on crisp mornings in a way not done since their fluffy hawklets began insisting on quick service and plenty of it. Crows who do not migrate get all enthused over a few warm October days and start building nests with boisterous gusto in two or three sites at once.

There are occasional dawns about the end of September whose bird choruses can give you an overwhelming illusion of May. After weeks of quiet, an unlooked-for excitement and eagerness make themselves felt. Early on September 26th last, I arose to take a short walk. The air seemed full of music: Phœbes were calling as if they had just arrived north, Bluebirds warbled, Robins were singing lustily, several Brown Thrashers "kissed" and darted about in the shrubbery, a dozen Song Sparrows at once were doing their cheerful best, a White-eyed Vireo went over his repertoire, a flock of Starlings made merry in the top of a locust tree, all the despised English Sparrows in the neighborhood were entertaining nest-building thoughts with unrepressed glee, Blue Jays and Red-shouldered Hawks interchanged, and a number of young Goldfinches tackled the family song-lesson along the brook. Blindfolded, one would have sworn he was hearing the spring roundelay again.

Considering that it was but two hundred centuries ago that this locality began emerging from the last Ice Age, it is not surprising that the seasons get somewhat confused. Either the axis of earth was much more inclined to its orbit than now; or there was an extraordinary displacement of the sun towards one "end" of that orbit; so that earth, slower moving when farthest away, suffered long and colder winters. Either cause, or both combined, might have brought on our series of five or six recurrent glacial epochs, during which epochs our latitude had nothing but winter. Antedating our last ice epoch, there certainly have been millenniums when the earth "stood up" a little straighter, at which times there was less accentuation of seasons and mild winters. Wild life appears to remember, in a dim instinctive way, that last Golden Age and, in many instances, is clearly puzzled by the new seasons. It has not become completely adapted to Cenozoic customs of climate, even though to such recent immigrants as ourselves, the seasons in our sectors seem as established as the framework of the universe. But the lowly vegetable and animal aboriginals recall deep in their protoplasm that not so long ago, as Time's ages run, temperate zone climates were not the well-ordered, four-course rounds they are now. In autumn, more especially, vestigial effects of ancient days are noticeable.

The evergreen Conifers cast their roots deeper than the subsoil of today, reaching backward even to the Carboniferous Era when trees first appeared and earth's perpetual summer required no shedding of leaves. Therefore they keep uselessly, though beautifully, evergreen in obstinate defiance of modern times. Bird migration, as well as the habit of leaf-shedding by deciduous trees, is also largely a relic of other days and other climes—even of other geographies. Some flocks are known to steer by islands which have sunk, forests which have disappeared and promontories that no longer rise above the sea.

Less striking maladjustments are not uncommon. We have picked blossoms of dwarf cornel in October, violets in October and November, and have heard hylas peeping lustily two weeks before Christmas—either three months early or seven months late. Chickweed blooms in every month in some northern states. Skunk cabbage, most restless of winter sleepers, wakes when the snow sheet is first snatched off in February, and often bores up through the dead leaves in October. Nearly everyone is familiar with the settled habit of witch-hazel in blooming in November, as though its life cycle had run down like a clock and needed rewinding. A whole row of red maples along this very orchard fence burst into red mists of bloom during the first week of January a few winters ago. And the white lilacs came out. That same week mosquitoes appeared mysteriously in the woods and the busy "sap flies" of maple-sugar time became very numerous, although a foot of snow had not long before blanketed the country-side. Spiders spun webs busily as if they had merely been waiting for business to pick up. A little gray-blue moth of the woods (Lycæna ladon) is the most sensitive thermometer of all; it is set to get out and flutter on a few hours no-tice. Hepatica sometimes salutes warm Octobers with blooms. The autumn of 1930 produced a second brood of tomato worm larvæ and an as-tonishing misfit family of seven juvenile red squirrels were captured on September 28th.

That tiresome annual "first robin" controversy, rises to questions of veracity simply because a few robins, who elect to stay north all winter, incau-tiously show themselves in a public place near the end of that season. Bluebirds, in transports of April sentimentality, often pass sobbing overhead until New Year's. In 1927-28 they warbled by during every week of the winter! . . . Instead of Spring-in-the-Fall being definitely on the calen-dar, it is, rather, a moveable season which can begin any time after the middle of September.

Spring-in-the-Fall, like Youth-in-the-Forties, has both the unreality of a dream and a dream's revelation of the soul beneath that is loath to die:

> That April should be shattered by a gust,
> That August should be levelled by a rain,
> I can endure, and that the lifted dust
> Of man should settle to the earth again;
> But that a dream can die, will be a thrust
> Between my ribs forever of hot pain!

. . . Ah, well. Now the cows are milked, the berries picked, the hay cut. Year's at the spring! No, it is *not* always May—but it ought to be! When I was a Boy—and You, perchance—I spake as a Boy and whistled as a Boy; now when I am become a Man, I cannot wholly put away childish things. No more can the Year!

Part Two

WE BECOME BETTER ACQUAINTED

A Liberal Education in Nature-craft

IN this day and generation when nearly every hopeful Jack and Jill expects to climb College Hill to get his or her pail of water from the well of knowledge; or, failing that, takes a correspondence course; or, acutely realizing later that they wish they had done either, they set about digesting some of the ambrosia dully named Adult Education; there seems to be no valid reason why nature-study should not attain to the dignities of a course and a curriculum. That being so, the author offers a beginning along these lines. Obviously, the scheme presents some minor difficulties; the more important one being that such work is largely a "laboratory course." (Logs outdoors aplenty—but no Mark Hopkins on one end!) It surely demands personal participation if ever a subject did—*and* a textbook. A book like the present volume is no place for an expanded treatment of such a proposal. It hasn't the space, for one thing.

So we give only in outline a set of topics which, mastered and enjoyed, entitle the matriculant in the great University of All Outdoors to his advanced degrees. The idea solicits your tolerance as well as your interest.

Would it not be putting the cart before the horse—or rather, the muffler before the fan—to expect a person to work out for himself beforehand a list of the things he *does not know about,* in order that he may seek them out? He probably wouldn't be able to do it for himself. Secondly, it is not the usual practice for the nature-lover to combine various and several branches of outdoor observation in his major hobby. And, thirdly, even if it be another evidence of human frailty, it is more competitive, hence more satisfactory, to compare one's attainments with the standard set by some other biped's accomplishment, so to exult in triumph or to extend oneself in rivalry. Therefore, we present such a list; make it cover as wide a scope as possible, and in it provide a rough standard of comparative rarity as regards each topic suggested.

It is expected, nay urged, that each topic be the subject of reading in the three-score-and-ten excellent nature books that have been approved of today. (A selected group of them appears at the end of this book.) If in one's walks and wades he looks with a vision sharpened by expectation, guided by probability and widened by reading, he will see much more than with the untrained eye. And, having seen, he may check up his findings against what others have observed in their meanderings.

The checking-up list which follows cannot escape sharp criticism from post graduates of the University of All Outdoors. Of this, the compiler is sure. It will be too commonplace, too difficult, too short, too long, too local, too inclusive, too cut-and-dried, too simple, too didactic, too popular, etc., etc. Since every curriculum, from Menes on the Nile to Montessori in Rome, likewise was and is criticized, why should one not expect this to be?

Five hundred points from a list should entitle the scholar to his respective Degree.

THE BACHELOR DEGREE

Credits

The mating "Song" of the Woodcock	30
A Humming Bird's nest	30
A laying of Turtle eggs	10
Finding Fringed Gentian in flower	5
Migrating Loons passing over	5
The "thunder pump" of the American Bittern	10
The Ant Lion at work	10
Watching one of the Giant Silkworm Moths emerge from cocoon	20

Credits

Migrating Fox Sparrows in song.	5
Learning how the Katydid talks.	10
A Praying Mantis and its egg-cases.	10
Finding a "Mud Puppy".	10
A Lady Slipper Orchid.	5
Egg of a wild bird not laid in any nest.	15
Water Arum in bloom.	5
Observing the Bartramian Sandpiper at home. . .	10
The Walking-stick Insect.	5
Identifying five species of Turtles.	15
Family of young Owls after leaving the nest. . .	25
A wild plant blooming each month of the year. .	20
Litter of baby Brown Hares in their fur-lined home	15
Learning to call 20 trees by "their first names"	10
Identifying five kinds of Galls	10
A Snake in act of swallowing Toad, Frog, Bird, Mouse, etc.	10
An Oven-bird's nest.	15
Locating a Weasel den.	15
Chimney Swift's nest not in a chimney.	25
Clutch of eggs upon which snow has fallen	20
Distinguishing ten species of edible Mushrooms or Fungi	15
"Hatching" and raising Toads or Frogs or Sala-manders	10
Hiving and keeping a swarm of wild Bees.	15
Flock of Red Crossbills in winter.	10
Year round census of a deserted old barn.	15

Credits

Identifying Olive-backed, Gray-cheeked, Hermit
and Wilson Thrushes   15
Collecting 20 Cocoons and having most of them
yield adults   10
Finding a fern "prothallium" or "seed"   10
Maintaining a homemade, self-stocked aquarium
for six months   15
Capturing a 'Possum   10
Knowing half a dozen Spiders and their webs. .   10
Domesticating a family of wild White-footed
Mice   5
Learning three species of Moles and a Shrew. . .   10
Capturing five kinds of common Snakes.   10
Learning ten wild tracks in the snow.   10
Spring flowers blooming in autumn.   5
Observing a migration of Monarch Butterfly. . .   15
Finding and cooking Morels, a spring fungus. .   10
Catching a Glow-worm   5
Seeing a family of Red Foxes.   10
Making a Christmas or New Year's Bird Census   10
A Bat found in the day-time.   5

THE MASTER DEGREE

Finding a litter of young Porcupines.   60
An example of Bird or Animal Albinism   40
A Blue Heron or Egret Colony.   50
Capturing a Spade-foot Toad.   50
Capturing, or raising, and domesticating any large
wild animal or game bird.   50
Membership in a local nature society.   30

Credits

Membership in a sectional or national organization	50
Appointment as a "Bird bander" by U. S. Biological Survey	75
Collecting 75 varieties of minerals and identifying them	100
Maintaining an ant-hill indoors over the winter	25
Finding every species of tree and shrub probably native to your county	100
Finding every species of batrachian probably native to your county	100
Publishing two magazine articles on a nature-lore subject	50
Mastering a list of 200 insects by identification in the field	100
A list of 350 species of plants	100
A list of 30 ferns	75
A list of all the *reptilia* probable to your county	100
A representative collection of Indian relics	75
Collecting at least 75 kinds of birds' nests	25
Making 100 photographs of wild life	50
Conducting a group or class in a season's outdoor study	50
Adding a species hitherto unrecorded in a given area	50
Personally identifying all species of Bats probable in your county	100
Personally identifying all Moles and Shrews probable in your county	75

THE DOCTORATE DEGREE

Accomplishing some such important piece of scientific nature work as reporting a species, sub-species or variety of animal or plant hitherto unrecorded; contributing some important article to a scientific biological publication; publishing a book on some phase of nature; or accumulating an exhaustive collection of specimens in some line of biology.

A BEGINNER'S COURSE IN INSECTS

Suppose that one desires to "major" in insects: for such a specialized "course" the author suggests the following as an outline.

One scarcely realizes, until he is launched into insect study, how baffling it is to locate in its correct order and family a strange specimen. But, after a bit of practice in specimen examination and memorizing, he ought to be able to get the orders straight, at least, and place an insect in one at sight. When he is sufficiently skilled to orient his Orders into Families and sub-Families, the coast is clear ahead of him. The table on pp. 94 and 95 is designed to be helpful to a beginner because of the range covered and the inclusion of so many common—and interesting—varieties. It is a check-list of common varieties in the northeastern section of the United States: "fifty insects you should know."

The list represents a target to aim at during your first season or two of attention to insects. A notebook record showing how, where and when you found and identified each of the species, will be a modest but adequate introduction to a nature-lover's kind of entomology. At the end of the book is a list of insect books to refer to for making identifications.

A BEGINNER'S COURSE IN PLANTS

Assuming your bent runs to flora rather than to fauna: on pp. 96 and 97 is a check-list of a few common species more or less common north of Philadelphia between June 15th and September 1st. These are "fifty summer plants you should know."

If you will use a new notebook—one which seems fairly to cry for something to be written on its white expanses—and upon the first fifty pages write the headings below, so that you may make record of your first finding of the species; you will presently have a start in wild flower botany which will launch you well on the road to mastery of the entire flora of your locality. At the end of the book is a list of books on wild flowers, tried and reliable, to be used in making your identifications.

Preferred Name	Scientific Label	Insect Order	Family or Sub-family
Glow Worm	Photuris pennsylvanica	Coleoptera	Lampyrinæ
Firefly	Photinus (several species)	Coleoptera	Lampyrinæ
Tree Borer	Tremex columba	Hymenoptera	Ichneumonoidea
Tree Borer parasite	Megarhyssa	Hymenoptera	Ichneumonoidea
Praying Mantis	Stagmomantis carolina	Orthoptera	Mantidæ
Walking Stick	Manomera blatchleyi	Orthoptera	Phasmidæ
Ant-lion	Myrmeleonia	Neuroptera	Myrmeleonidæ
Aphis-lion	Chrysopa	Neuroptera	Chrysopidæ
Mud Wasp	Sceliphron	Hymenoptera	Sphecidæ
Bald-faced Hornet	Vespa maculata	Hymenoptera	Vespidæ
Yellow Jacket	Vespa germanica	Hymenoptera	Vespidæ
Spittle Insect	Cercopida	Hemiptera	Cercopidæ (several)
Caddis	Halesus argus (et al)	Trichoptera	
May Beetle	Phyllophaga	Coleoptera	Scarabæidæ
Cabbageworm Butterfly	Pieris rapæ*	Lepidoptera	Papilionidæ
Monarch Butterfly	Anosia plexippus	Lepidoptera	Nymphalidæ
Cecropia Moth	Samia cecropia	Lepidoptera	Saturniidæ
Polyphemus Moth	Telea polyphemus	Lepidoptera	Saturniidæ
Luna Moth	Actias luna	Lepidoptera	Saturniidæ
Promethea Moth	Callosamia promethea	Lepidoptera	Saturniidæ
Cynthia Moth	Philosamia cynthia	Lepidoptera	Saturniidæ
Katydid	Pterophylla camellifolia	Orthoptera	Tettigoniidæ
Summer Cicada	Tibicina septendecim	Hemiptera	Cicadidæ
Common Grasshopper	Locustinæ (several sp.)	Orthoptera	Acrididæ

Common Name	Species	Order	Family
Dragon Fly	Anax junius (et al)	Odonata	Aeschnidæ, etc. (three)
Damsel Fly	Hetærina, etc.	Odonata	Lasiocampidæ
Tent Caterpillar	Malacosoma americana	Lepidoptera	Ephemeridæ
May Fly	Ephemera varia	Plectoptera	Gerridæ
Water Strider	Gerris remigis	Hemiptera	Gyrinidæ
Whirligig Beetle	Gyrinus	Coleoptera	Membracidæ
Tree Hopper	(Several species)	Hemiptera	Aphididæ
Rose Aphis	Aphis mali	Hemiptera	Corydalidæ
Dobson Fly	Corydalis cornuta	Neuroptera	Papilionidæ
Tiger Swallowtail	Papilio glaucus	Lepidoptera	Nymphalidæ
Silver-spot Butterfly	Argynnis aphrodite	Lepidoptera	Tabanidæ
Deer Fly	Chrysops	Diptera	Simuliidæ
Black Fly	Simulium meridionale	Diptera	Chironomidæ
Midge (Punkie)	Culicoides	Diptera	Psychidæ
Bag-worm	Thridopteryx ephemeræformis	Lepidoptera	Arctiidæ
Woolly Bear	Isia isabella	Lepidoptera	Criocerini
Potato Beetle	Leptinotarsa	Coleoptera	Coreidæ
Squash Bug	Anasa tristis	Hemiptera	Coccinellidæ
Lady Beetle	(Many species)	Coleoptera	Elateridæ
Skip Jack Beetle	(Several species)	Coleoptera	Silphidæ
Burying Beetle	Necrophorus marginatus	Coleoptera	(Hormomyia)
Witch-hazel Gall Fly	Hormaphis hamamelidis	Diptera	Cynipidæ
Oak Gall Fly	Amphibolips confluentus	Hymenoptera	
Eur. Corn-borer	Pyralid nubilalis*	Lepidoptera	Bombidæ
Bumblebee	(Several species)	(Suborder: Apoidea)	Sphinginæ
Tomato-worm	Phlegethontius carolina	Lepidoptera	

* Species introduced from abroad.

Preferred Name	Other Common Names	Plant Family
Tawny Hawkweed *	Paintbrush Hawkweed. Orange Hawkweed †	Composite
Canada Hawkweed *	Paintbrush Hawkweed. Yellow Hawkweed †	Composite
Butterfly Weed †	Pleurisy-root	Milkweed
Common Milkweed †		Milkweed
Ragged Robin *	Cuckoo Flower	Pink
Showy Lady's Slipper	Moccasin Flower Pink	Orchid
Yellow Lady's Slipper	Yellow Moccasin Flower	Orchid
Wild Ginger †		Birthwort
Pitcher Plant †		Pitcher Plant
Venus Fly-trap	Round-leaved Sundew	Sundew
Jewel-weed †	Spotted Touch-me-not	Jewelweed
Viper's Bugloss *	Blueweed	Borage
Toad-flax *	Butter-and-eggs	Figwort
Mullein *	Great Mullein	Figwort
Moth Mullein		Figwort
Purple Gerardia		Figwort
Turtle-head		Figwort
Painted Cup		Figwort
Wild Carrot *	Queen Anne's Lace. Bird's Nest	Parsley
Cow Parsnip		Parsley
Cardinal Flower		Lobelia
Closed Gentian	Bottle Gentian	Gentian
Indian Pipe	Corpse Plant. Ghost Flower	Pyrola (or Heath)
Pipsissewa	Prince's Pine	Pyrola (or Heath)
Boneset	Thoroughwort	Composite

White Snakeroot		Composite
Joe-Pye-Weed	Trumpetweed (?)	Composite
Robin's Plantain	Spring Daisy	Composite
Elecampane *		Composite
Ragweed		Composite
Cone-flower	Black-eyed Susan †	Composite
Ten-petal Sunflower	(Many varieties)	Composite
Hemp Nettle *	Stinging Nettle	Mint
Nightshade *	Bittersweet (?)	Nightshade
Lamb's-quarters *	Pigweed	Goosefoot
Shepherd's Purse *		Mustard
Chicory *		Composite
Tansy *		Composite
Oswego Tea	Bee Balm	Mint
Wild Bergamot		Mint
Bouncing Bet *	Soapwort	Pink
Mandrake	May-apple (flowers in May)	Barberry
Blue Vervain		Vervain
Ladies' Tresses		Orchid
Pickerel Weed		Pickerel Weed
Polypoddy Fern		(Fern)
Cinnamon Fern		(Fern)
Interrupted Fern		(Fern)
Maidenhair Fern		(Fern)
Christmas Fern		(Fern)

* Introduced from abroad.
† Discussed in the next chapter.

Some Plant Notables

THAT there is no accounting for tastes is one of the oldest sayings of mankind. Whether a rose is finer than a lily is, of course, not a debatable question. Certain enthusiasms of mine have from time to time flowered into whole pages in my notebooks and I have reproduced them here simply for what they are: personal reactions concerning some plants I have especially noticed and liked. Whether a reader would be equally interested, I have no idea. This characteristic and that, this color or another, the particular setting in which they have grown—all these have probably gone into my liking, and I attempt no apology or explanation.

Many a flower is born to blush unsung just because its name is not musical: poets have unwittingly made others into universal favorites. It was inevitable, as soon as it acquired its name, that the Twisted Eglantine should become a darling of the poets. And it was quite as foretellable that the drably christened Fringed Milkwort was doomed to a Cinderella existence, never to come to the ballrooms of the rich nor to the pages of the bards. Emerson was able to place the Wild Azalea among the immortals because, fortunately, it had another cognomen in the ancient family name of Rhodora, whose "beauty is its own excuse for being." Yellow Adder's Tongues, or, as they are alternatively called, Dog-tooth Violets, could never dance like "hosts of yellow Daffodils"—on paper—although every nature-lover has felt his heart dance with them. Address the Pipsissewa by another name, Prince's Pine, and it will somehow smell more sweet.

The Namer of Names has been unfair. Contrast some random names: Violet, Columbine, Anemone, Rosemary, Hyacinth, with some whose owners are just as beautiful: Vetch, Hardhack, Dock, Loosestrife. It is a fortuitous thing that many American wild flowers bear aliases which are as attractive as the commoner names are repelling. Moneywort may be dubbed Myrtle in botanical good form; the exquisite Shinleaf is as well Pyrola; Cowslips are really Marigolds. . . . Yes, we are more intrigued by the melody of a name than by the flower itself. Strict botanists will insist that much eulogy in print given to Wild Thyme, Primrose, Hawthorn and Eglantine is hardly justifiable to a naked eye. Something of the blue

Mediterranean and its vine-clad slopes must have got deep into the minds of people who could speak of Helianthus, Chrysanthemum, Calendula, Arethusa, Lobelia and Rhododendron; while surely the laconic rigorous north speaks out bluntly in such words as Dog-bane, Bedstraw, Dandelion, Poke and Huckleberry.

Here is the nosegay I am placing before you; a bouquet taken, as it were, from pressed specimens left between the notebook pages.

Black-eyed Susan—Most of the weeds of our New England fields—by "weeds" we mean plants that are easy to raise and impossible to eradicate—are imports from Europe. The list is long; somewhere Burroughs lists about twenty-five of the commonest, most persistent pests, as Old World migrants: Mullein, plantain, dock, mustard, dandelion, ragweed, purslane, etc. But there is with us in the East one perennial weed that has attempted retaliation; a Lochinvar come out of the American West. As if the harassed New England farmer was not beset with enough vexations, his fields are assailed from the rear. Indeed, the Westerner is carrying the war into the enemy's country, invading England and Europe already—and not alone by way of flower gardens, but also by a strategy similar to that which gained Troy, the horse in the case being exported hay.

The Black-eyed Susan (Rudbeckia hirta) is the invader. It has also been most unthrillingly named Cone Flower, in allusion to its central floret-disk. Golden-yellow, rich madder purple: it is doubtful if there is a flower more gorgeous, more tropically raimented than this in our latitude. And it is everywhere to be seen for the looking; to be picked for the picking. It will come to you almost at a gesture; but will not depart even after a campaign.

Jewel-weed—When Australian farmers tried to introduce American red clover, to grow it as fodder, they were puzzled by the fact that, although good crops resulted the first year, it did not come up vigorously again the following spring. It soon petered out altogether. Try as they might, red clover simply would not seed itself over the mild Australian "winter." Long experimenting finally demonstrated that the burly American bumble-bee should have been imported along with the clover. In its native land, however slightly the farmer holds the bumble-bee, the presence of that buzzing buccaneer makes his clover crop possible. By carrying pollen from flower-head to flower-head, and it is the only insect perfectly adapted to the task, the bee causes the seed to be properly cross-fertilized. Australia imported American bumble-bees, and ever after she has "lived in clover."

More recently, another instance showing the strict dependence of plants upon the pollen-carriers of its native habitat, has come to light. Jewel-weed is one of our most charming wild flowers. Because of the orchid-like blossom; rich yellow, spotted with red; it is locally named "Wild Lady's Slipper." Its odd cornucopia shape makes it highly adapted to thrusts from the humming bird's bill which is almost the sole means of its pollen's being carried to other flowerets. As if distrusting itself, however, and having premonitions that possibly humming birds would not be with it always, the plant developed the expedient of growing, later in the season, closed (cleistogamous) flowers which never open, and which are self-pollinated, producing seeds without blooming. When introduced into England as a decorative plant to fringe garden pools and streams, it missed its compatriot humming bird—there being none of this bird family outside the Americas. What transpired? The reliant little Jewel-weed proceeded to enlarge upon its auxiliary manner of seed making;

and is reported by English botanists as being dependent upon this means alone.

As for the seeds, what youngster does not call Jewel-weed "Touch-Me-Not" on account of its elastic, jumpy little seed pods which explode when the detonating-cap, so to speak, is touched ever so lightly? Up through the inside of the seed pod a remarkable tensioned fibre extends, and this snaps back into a coiled spring upon the least jar or at a touch on the outer tip, ripping the pod open and shooting the seeds several feet. *Impatiens biflora* is truly an *impatient* vegetable; resourceful, artistic, prolific.

Witch-hopple—It is strange how very few "from the outside"—as we Adirondackers call other people—have been privileged to view one of the sights of our northern mountain forests, the Witch-hopple shrub in bloom. May's first three weeks cover the flowering period, and at that season—just before the dreaded blackfly appears— few "outsiders" chance to visit the mountains.

Moose Wood is another name commonly applied to Witch-hopple; the first because of what it does for moose and deer; the second for what it does for the woods walker. In winter the meaty, large budded branches just reaching above the snow furnish particularly good browsing for the deer tribe; in summer its zigzagging manner of growth, mainly knee-high, and its burden of large thick leaves, make it a constant and exasperating hindrance to easy tramping through the woods.

But before the leaves unfold, for nearly a month it fills the wilderness with lavish splendor. Fame has come to the Rhododendron and to the Laurel, which flood a countryside with a pink-and-whiteness almost too tropical for the reserved, un-impulsive flora of the north. But no one has sung the Moose Wood. In flat, crowded panicles of creamy whiteness, its flowers stretch away as far as one can see between the unleaved trees, keeping a certain gleaming level, looking like a froth-covered tide, ebbing limitlessly among the primeval weatherbeaten giants of the forest. Half-closed eyes give one the illusion of a spring snowfall, so unbroken is the white stratum that tops the undergrowth.

Later the stocky leaves appear, the forest floor is no longer bare and easily scrutinized from above, but may harbor vital secrets under the flat shield of its foliage. Deer, otter, mink, porcupine, fox, and even black bruin when he chooses, may lie or slip about with a shade less alertness.

The Paint-Brush Hawkweeds—They do look like worn-out paint brushes, played-out, flaring, steeped in once-used bright pigments. But it never occurred to me to wonder as to the origin of the name Hawkweed until last spring, when I noticed a number of dried gray flower stalks of the previous summer's growth used in the lining material of a red-shouldered hawk's nest. Soon afterward another hawk's eerie to which I climbed made similar use of these stalks. Then, upon "reading up" about this peculiarity, I found other birds' nesters had made note occasionally of the same thing. No one as yet offers to account for it. May we possibly have here the origin of the name applied to the three varieties of hawkweeds that have immigrated into the country to the regret of Eastern farmers?

My field notes also revealed the fact that two nests of the White-rumped Shrike (or Butcher Bird) showed many of the weed-stems in the second or middle section of the cup. Shrikes' nests in this part of the State, always built in thornapple (or Black Haw) bushes, have outside frameworks of strong twigs and innermost lining of feathers, while the transition or body of the cup is made of straws, rootlets, stalks—and, in these two instances—many Hawkweed stems.

The flame-colored Orange Hawkweed, once a flower garden pet, and its near relative, the buttercup-tinted Yellow Hawkweed, in spite of their once pampered existence, have not "lost the common touch" but remain natural, unpretentious democrats, never invading rich-soil fields, but only common, poor, thin pastures. In many an eastern American state they have largely crowded out better cattle forage—oh, but how beautiful they are, singly or in mass! The cows' loss is the eyes' gain. The so-called Field Hawkweed, a variety that avoids not the fattest of soils, is the most detested interloper. If we could but entice back again into the preserves of the posy garden, many native "weeds"—which, by the way, are of insignificant infamy compared to the scores of introduced weeds—the crops, but not the landscape, would be the better for it.

Milkweeds—Whenever, in a state of nature, we find a number of plants closely alike in size and form, but each differently colored, there is something particularly appealing in the set-like arrangement. Especially is this true when the coloration is a solid one; say an allover yellow or red or white. Such an assortment is not at all common —except where scientists have been working in collusion with Nature. They have evolved variegated sets of cats, dogs, cattle, fowls, guinea pigs, rabbits, etc., and given us examples among the gladiolas and irises.

There is a satisfying natural instance of this peculiarity among the midsummer Milkweeds (Asclepius). Perhaps, in a single meadow, if one be lucky, he may find three or four species: Common Milkweed (Asclepius syriaca), "Purple" Milkweed (A. purpurascens), Poke Milkweed (A. phytolaccoides) and Butterfly-weed (A. tuberosa). The first is lilac-to-lavender-brown, the second dull crimson, the third ivory-white, the last an exquisite orange. Beside these four, there are to be sought and identified the rarer *Verticillata*, bearing greenish-white flowers; *Quadrifolia*, with magenta ones; and *Incarnata* whose blooms are pink. The Milkweeds all belong to a world-wide rubber-producing family.

All the Milkweeds (but one) possess a milky juice which oozes from stems and leaves at the least puncture by insects. The white juice becomes sticky at once, and discourages a climbing predatory ant, whose foot-hooks would actually puncture the plant when merely walking up it. The characteristic Milkweed pods in autumn, stuffed with tufts of silky fluff, were used in the old days as mattress and pillow stuffing. As objects of indoor decoration all winter through, they add a rare touch. (In her book, *Nature's Garden*, Neltje Blanchan gives a most entertaining account of the encounters of insects with the Milkweeds' pollen mechanism.)

Wild Ginger—One of those indefinably queer plants to be put into the mental catalogue along with the four next following. Mrs. W. S. Dana calls it a "vegetable crank." Its root-stock is not the source of commercial ginger, nor does it taste just like it, although similar. The root and strange flower destined it to be the prey of the pharmaceutical botanists of the last century. To these magicians the odor, taste or appearance of any plant suggested medicinal applications, and such imagined virtues soon crystallized into certainty. Innocent little herbs became specifics in recipes for all manner of human complaints: witness snake-root, toothwort, fever-few, boneset, etc. Wild Ginger's particular field as a remedy was wide. It was touted for nearly every uncomfortable feeling from snake-bite to deafness. But in strict fact, it is an unobtrusive root-and-branch-and-all-in-all, minding its own business of growing, a heartsease only to nature-lovers.

A striking contrast: vigorous upstanding leaves on thick hearty stems, and a cowering muddy-purple blossom of which it seems unaccountably ashamed. That blossom, a tiny three-sided cup opening groundward, green from above, looks as if it just barely came within the name "flower." There are few other plants in which leafage and bloom are so estranged; and, except for certain orchids, few whose flowers, unclothed by leaf, petals or bract, seem thus to spring from their roots. After all, the flower does not play much part in reproducing the species, for Ginger spreads in widening circles by budding from radiating roots, rather than by seeding itself. Probably this is the reason why its distribution is so localized. The plant does not care for sun, blooms early, is likely to be mistaken at first glance for a violet, and where once located is always to be found.

The Water Arum—It will remind you of the Calla Lily, just as it has reminded so many others who have found it in some shaded swamp. It is a not unworthy country cousin of the magnificent Calla of the city florist. Its perfect immaculateness amid mud and stagnant water is most suggestive to those whose minds run to parable. This suggestiveness is further emphasized by the clean luxuriance of the rich green leaves and stems. Only one other plant exhibits such surpassing purity, dazzling amid surroundings as unlovely— the white Water Lily, who "counts the still, hot hours like beads"—but Calla lacks the lavish cloying scent of the Water Lily that dwells in still but not stagnant waters.

You must seek in July for *calla palustris*, sometimes called the water Calla Lily, the lily which is *not* a lily; the calla which is *not* a true calla; the flower which is *not* a flower at all, but only a bract!

Indian Pipe—Some plants have "gone wrong"; they have imitated the animals in becoming parasitic upon ready-made food: vegetation and flesh. The whole group known as fungi have thus retrograded from green self-sufficiency to anemic paleness. Here and there in otherwise healthy and orthodox plant families are individual species turned degenerate: dodder is one, sundew another, cancer-root a third. Indian Pipe is the most striking of the lot; a white ghost plant sucking juices and products of bacterial decay from tree roots and rotting wood. Sometimes the beautiful-shaped stalks are salmon color—perhaps due to a peculiarity of its food.

For years I felt so sure the delicate things would not endure bringing home that I did not try it. Exposed to the light very long they blacken and shrivel. But now I know that if wrapped and kept from drying out on the way, the flowers last for a long time in a vase; though this fact seems to contradict several botanists. The flower reverses a habit common to most in that it bends downward before being fertilized, but points upward as the ovary starts to develop. . . . Indian Pipe is reported to be distributed over most of the United States wherever there are cool shady woods. I have found it in bloom on the summit of Slide Mountain, whose altitude of 4,208 feet is the highest point in the Catskills.

Pitcher Plant—Doubt exists as to whether this "carnivorous" vegetable gets any important fraction of its sustenance from the luckless insects caught in its pitchers. These victims seem to undergo a certain digestion there, and inasmuch as no other explanation appears to account for the astonishing adaptation of the leaves, we may well conclude that it lives in part on animal proteins. The pitcher-like leaves hold a drowning fluid; the walls of the pitcher are set with stiff downward-pointing hairs to keep the struggler down; and some of these hairs exude a sweet liquor as a bait; so why question that the whole intent of the plant is kill and eat insects? Above these abbatoirs stands a splendidly esthetic blossom, odd in shape, brilliant in coloring, delicate in scent,—a triumph of beauty created out of death! Thoreau said "I think we have no other plant so singular and remarkable." Sphagnum bogs or thoroughly sour swamps are its only habitat.

Skunk Cabbage—So common is this lush grower south of latitude 42 degrees that everyone knows it; so common that it does seem a pity no Burbank has arisen who could deodorize, or at least deacridize the thick succulent foliage so that cattle might browse on it. If a cow inadvertently eats a bit of it, her milk tells the story for a day or so. Even the roots are permeated the whole year round with the characteristic flavor. Its flower has a beauty all its own, and no plant holds its flower so long.

Here is a quotation from the writings of Clarence M. Weed, which presents a most interesting observation: "Upon a central stalk is a closely grouped cluster of flowers. Each cluster has two distinct stages of existence: in the first stage the pollen-bearing parts of the flower develop; in the second the seed-bearing parts develop. In any hood at any one time only one condition of the flowers is present . . . pollen from one hood must be carried to another. . . . [this was done] by small gnat-like flies." We used to call the latter "sap flies," because they so often got into the maple sap buckets in early March, when the crusted snow lay all about.

An interesting record to be made every year is the date on which the "new" plant pushes up into daylight. Since Skunk Cabbage is all out of tune with the seasons, that date will always appear *the year before*. I have even seen the monk's hood tips appearing on October 15th. From then on all through the winter, they will keep appearing here and there, as if impatiently peeping out to see why the snow and ice are not gone. Freezing has no effect at all upon the plant. In midsummer its fruit—it sounds odd to call it that—looks *tropical*, a big oval knot of a thing, nearly as hard as cocoa-nut shell. The enormous root-mass from which the flower and then the leaves spring annually will often fill a bushel basket, and its center is often two feet below the surface. Probably it is the earliest spring flower north of Mason-Dixon's Line.

Taming Wild Flowers

A DISGRUNTLED politician out our way is quoted as having said: "An expert is only an ordinary man a long way from home." This trenchant judgment, it seems to me, neatly sums up mankind's usual indifference, if not contempt, for the familiar and the usual, right in one's neighborhood. How calmly we Americans pass by our amazing skyscrapers to rush across the sea and fall prostrate before famous pieces of Old World architecture not a whit more difficult to construct and no more beautiful—in their own way—than our recent city masterpieces.

Like skyscrapers, our native wild flowers are only just being noticed. Garden enthusiasts, following the lead of experts in their line, are at last beginning to add some of these so-called simple flowers of the countryside to their cultivated pets. The word "simple" is in itself a patronizing epithet, for if you stop to think about it a moment, you realize that it means *common*, and nothing else.

However, as we have said, the great majority

of our garden flowers—and vegetables, too—are
common and wild in some part of the world. Fully
thirty plants regularly regarded as weeds in the
United States, are, in Europe, domesticated denizens of gardens. And twice that number of our
weeds were weeds there, too; taking to their new
habitat here with passionate liking. As for our cultivated flowers (many of which also are of foreign
origin), we often prize them more for their exotic
quality than for their loveliness. Dozens of natives that are certainly the peers of these falsely
treasured aliens are passed by.

Floricultural snobbishness is by no means exclusively an American trait. In my trips to New
Zealand, for instance, I have seen whole land-
scapes decorated by the Nasturtium, which is native there, but never found it planted in gardens;
nor, apparently, was it gathered for bouquets any
oftener than our Goldenrod is. The New Zealand
show has often recalled to me that wonderful
twin display of our own summer fields: Viper's
Bugloss and Toad-flax. This blue-purple-yellow-
orange combination, now riotous in many eastern
sections (although both plants are Europeans)
produces one of the most striking color shows in
America—yet I doubt if either of them, not to say
both together, are used in our dooryards at all.

They might well be—just as Nasturtiums are.

Now, I write these lines as a nature-lover and not as a floral expert. I am well aware that recent catalogues from nurseries offer an extensive list of common woodland flowers, although I notice that the publishers are sometimes canny about stressing the fact of their commonness. Our three most widespread Trilliums, or Wake Robins, seem to have come into their own, and so have even Adder's Tongue, Hepatica, and others. So the trend is started already—at least, for the specialists and experts. It does them credit.

But as a nature-lover, the point I want to stress is that taming wild flowers is a little-done, yet outstandingly fascinating feature of one's out-of-doors' hobby. It is an intimate link connecting nature and the home, one which perennially revives memories of companions and experiences on long-past excursions. Scarcely a lover of nature but will pluck wild blossoms and bring them back to his vases; but few, I find, think of transplanting their roots and making a wild garden of them at home.

From the very nature of things, wild flowers are either perennials or ready growers from their scattered seeds. If they weren't, they would not have been able to maintain themselves in the struggle beyond the fences. Therefore, a wood's garden is a long-term satisfaction, a year-to-year reminder of one's walks and finds. Just as surely as you will find a great deal more of delight in the aquarium which you collect for and stock yourself than in the make-believe Nature outfit bought at the shops; so also is the delight in the plantings which you discover in your rambles. You come to realize that with the few rootlings you have carried home you have brought back the whole countryside with you to be your solace and record.

The enduring persistency of some of our wild flowers is remarkable. The first effort I ever made toward bringing permanent mementoes home to plant was when I was about ten years old. I developed quite a flourishing little nook. Three years later we moved from the old ancestral place, and I did not see it again for at least six years. I recall vividly how affecting it was to find most of the by-gone and deserted little friends still struggling valiantly with grass and weeds in the spot where I had set them so long before! . . . At our present location, I have some lusty Jack-in-the-Pulpits, whose remote ancestors we brought in and set eight Aprils ago.

Somehow, the keenest edge on this hobby seems to be whetted in early spring. Perhaps this is due to the general all-round planting activity that arises and demands action in April; and perhaps to the utter irresistibleness of the first few wood's blossoms. At all events, I can hardly keep my children from bringing in great loads of things which we have no proper place for; and, as for myself, I *feel* the same desire on every spring walk. I am sure that if Skunk Cabbage did not have roots which go down almost to the geological center of the globe, we should have borders and beds of them all around the place, so appealing do we find its quaint blooms when they start coming out in February and March. (But, of course, this plant demands a place which is very damp all summer through.)

So it seems appropriate that the beginner's efforts along these lines should start with April. Here is a short list of wild plants that can be transplanted. It does not include all that I have tried, nor all that the professionals' catalogues offer. But it will suffice for a start: Wood Anemone, Hepatica, Jack-in-the-Pulpit, Wild Geranium, the Trilliums, Cowslip, Columbine, Squirrel-corn, Dutchman's Breeches, Adder's Tongue, Sarsaparilla, False and True Solomon-seals, many Violets, Milkwort, Spring Beauty (Claytonia), Wild Iris. The latter does not bloom until May and June, but its leaves are in sight much earlier, and if you have a brook margin or any other spot likely to be damp all through the summer, it is a hardy sojourner.

To exile these unprotesting flowers from their native soil does not require that you delve into books for directions, nor possess any special knack at gardening: they are *naturalists'* flowers, not gardeners'. Speaking, again, not as an expert, I feel sure that if you observe nature's rules—i.e. reproduce as nearly as possible the conditions under which you find them growing, your luck with them will suffice you. Note the details of shadiness, dampness, soil richness and depth of rootage; and then look overhead to imagine what the spot looks like in summer. Copy these features, and let nature take its course. The chief difficulty encountered will probably have to do with soil. Wood dirt cannot be manufactured to order, so the easiest thing to do is to bring back in baskets from the rich places the dirt for your own nooks. A certain number of wild shrubs and plants demand sour soil conditions: Rhododendron, Laurel and Hawk-weed, for instance, will not grow for you except in what gardeners call poor soil—a soggy, heavy ground lacking in lime and showing an acid reaction to litmus papers. Of course, such soil must be reproduced around your home. Nurserymen sell a liquid preparation especially designed to render any ground acid. Ten to one, however, you already have such situations in the shadier portions of your grounds.

If you are interested in ferneries, a most fascinating pursuit is to collect all the many varieties of ferns native to your locality. These flowerless plants, almost without exception, need plenty of moisture to thrive, and few of them will live in exposed sunny places. Perhaps you will be surprised at the extent of the underground root-mass which a fern has below it. Springing year after year from a semi-woody and spongy rootage, it grows for many a season at the same spot. So dig up plenty of bottom to your ferns, and when replanting them, make a deep and wide hole well reinforced with wood mould. The first season or two, artificial watering during dry spells will get them properly established. Few plant fanciers become familiar with the intimacies of fern life. Because they do not reproduce by means of flowers, but belong to a vegetable order older than seed bearers, and give birth to new plants by means of "spores," ferns are seemingly less dramatic in their life history. They do not appeal so strikingly to the casual botanist. But once you become initiated into their odd variations, one from another, and learn to identify a score or more by sight, they add greatly to one's quiet enjoyment of the woods. The earlier in the spring they are brought in, the better will be the chances of their standing the change of location.

The question of the best time of year for transplanting wild roots is not at all a vexatious one. The rule is: spring-flowerers early in spring; late flowerers in late autumn. With many plants it does not seem to matter much when you remove them, provided you are able to water them plentifully for several weeks afterward. However, when you come to shrubs and trees, there is no time better than just after the frost leaves the ground, unless it is just before hard frosts begin in October. The point to notice is that the season when the roots have begun to send out new tips and fresh branchings is naturally not a good time to break and bruise the infinitely tender things by wrenching them from their connections. Of course, if you are able to get out most of the underground ramifications intact, even this consideration does not preclude the continuance of their growth. Most wild shrubs and trees have two periods of root growth: May, and September-October. Many a sturdy sapling, so attractive in summer as to be irresistible to those who go into the woods at no other time, is doomed to death if taken up then. Often one notices them being hopefully brought home in the family automobile at the close of the summer vacation or at the end of a week-end jaunt, usually pulled up by main strength and allowed to endure the sunshine on the return trip! Such gambling on nature's sleight-of-hand is a waste of time, and closely borders on vandalism.

To return to wild flowers again. A little later in the year than suggested for the list given above, try your hand on Bouncing Bet, Turtle-head and Black-eyed Susan. They are especially showy and hardy. So are the later blooming Jerusalem Artichoke and Ten-petal Sunflower. Meadow Rue is likeable, too; a dainty tall plant, more admired for its foliage than its flowers. Butterfly Weed is undoubtedly one of the most beautiful of wild flowers, and one of the most difficult to transplant. After many experiments with this sister of the Milkweed family, I have concluded that there is only one safe way to get them from the meadows: jot down carefully the exact location of its flaming orange bloom—if you don't, you are sure to forget it—and, having tied a strip of cloth loosely around the stalks, go with your spade in early fall and carefully dig up the roots. No use to dig it up dur-

ing flowering time—at least, I have never succeeded with it thus—and before its flowers appear
you can never find a plant. That vegetable skyscraper, Joe Pye Weed, whose big magenta heads
blossom in August, can be developed in healthy
clumps almost anywhere that the ground is damp.
No matter if it is so common a weed, it is a splendid show if strategically placed as a background,
and the cut heads make a lasting indoor bouquet
as well. Lusty groups of fall's Purple Aster, and
even of Goldenrod, are not to be despised; provided you prevent them from going to seed or
spreading by means of underground stemming.
Wild or Hog Peanut is a pretty vine on a pole—
but beware of letting its roots spread!

If you have either a little brook on your land
or an artificial pool, your scope of wild flower
taming is widely enlarged. There are scores of
brook-lurking plants ready at hand. I have listed
Cowslip above—it is one of the earliest. I shall
not even attempt to list a group. All one needs to
do is to make expeditions up and down a stepping-
stone stream at different times during the year,
and take up from the soft mud anything that attracts him; delving into the flower books if need
be to learn their common names later. No plants
are easier to dig up. Jewel-weed is a most lush

beauty, sure to attract all the humming birds in the vicinity. The giant vigor of Water Parsnip appeals to some; the Dentarias and the Cardinal Flower, to everyone. Iron Weed is striking, both in flowering time and after. Bottle Gentian and its much rarer cousin, Fringed Gentian, need no recommendation. Both our Water Lilies, Yellow and White, grow well in large pools—but here I am afraid one must go to the bookshelves to be successful in perpetuating them from year to year. Lobelia is "true blue" wherever you can get it started; Oswego Tea, a lordly red most prosaically named. Our Wild Iris or Blue Flag grows much better by a stream than in a less wet locality.

On rocky ledges, not too exposed to summer sunshine, the exquisite saxifrage will greet April's warmth as eagerly as you will yourself. And Wild Lupine—until I glanced out my window just this moment to where my own little patch of it is thriving, I had quite forgotten to mention it!— once you get a few of its exceedingly deep delving roots to take hold in a sandy infertile patch of land, no matter how sunny, it will go on forever. Next to Butterfly Weed, it is perhaps the most delightful of natives. Like the former, it is hard to establish if moved when it is most conspicuous, and I recommend a somewhat similar plan for doing the trick—except that early spring is probably a better time than autumn.

After a few seasons of effort with some of the wild flowers mentioned in the preceding paragraphs, you will go on and on enlarging your experiences. Such prizes as Turk's Cap and Tiger Lilies, the lovely Blackberry Lily (which has migrated to us from the Orient via the garden), Robin's Plantain, Wood Betony, Painted Cup, and scores of others, will fall to your collecting basket. Maybe you will succeed with some of the Orchids, if your soil is right. The dainty Mitreworts will accompany you home. Before you realize it, you will find yourself an accomplished botanist, not to mention an able gardener.

Having formed the invariable habit of not going afield without an empty grape basket hung on your arm, you will rarely return without some addition to your collection. First of all, however, you have to divest the adjective "common" from its implications of worthlessness; and, like the animal tamer, learn to look every flower straight in the eye.

Then you will not unconsciously ask yourself, as so often the art snob does, "It's pretty; but is it art?" or "It's pretty; but is it rare?"—you will raise no question at all, but merely fall-to and bring it back with you because you like it.

To Tell the Age of a Tree

THE age of Pine, Spruce, Fir, Sassafras, and other trees which grow in a whorled manner, can usually be told at a glance by counting the successive nodes or stories of annual growth. Up to about twenty years this is an accurate process—beyond that, since yearly growth is then much slower, you may be confused. Every spring a new radiation of branches is put out from the terminal bud-cluster at the tip of the tree, and a new central spire shoots straight up, this by midsummer to be crowned with the next season's bud-cluster,—and so on. The most vigorous growth of such trees is apt to come between six and fifteen years of age.

Sometimes an accident, or the vandalism of a boring-insect, damaging the terminal upright growth, will cause the tree to call upon one of the normally radiating twigs to take the place of the true central one. An act which seems almost like a slow consciousness on the tree's part! As a result of such a substitution, a slight sidewise break in the vertical main trunk will be noticed; but if the count is followed up along the substitute trunk, nearly the same age will be arrived at as if the break had not occurred, although occasionally a year's growth or two is obscured at the point of accident.

Comparatively few trees, however, are of whorled growth; and for these others there is no means of close estimate by an amateur guesser. On rather young ones, should there be a branch out from the main stem near the ground, you may ascertain the age of that branch; and by adding say three years, you get a reasonably likely account of the tree's adolescence.

There is a pretty sure method of calculating branch or twig age on all trees. To start with a type of tree having fairly smooth bark, especially on its limbs, notice that the main stem of the branch or twig shows a yearly series of circular (or semi-circular) scars. These scars are left by the end-bud of the branch as the bud breaks out in spring and the new growth emerges. The scar is a slightly raised line in the bark, and such marking appears at quite regular intervals along the stem. The older the scar, the more obliterated it becomes. The number upon a stem is the yearly age of that stem, plus the final end-twig developing in the current season. A little practice will enable you to detect this so-called annual node (or scar) under the various guises in which it appears in different species.

Practically all trees, large and small, in temperate latitudes belong to one of the two grand divisions of plant classification. One division (Monocotyledons) has no representatives in tree form above the southern states; the other (Dicotyledons) includes our trees whose leaves show netted veins and whose trunks have all their sap-tubes in a ring in the inner bark. This ring is important for our purpose. Each year the trunk in expanding produces a new ring of tubes outside the old one. About the time, in late summer, when the new wood hardens, the newest sap-tubes get progressively smaller and smaller. That is why, when you look at a cross section of a trunk, you see alternate rings of porous and comparatively solid wood. The porous area shows the spring-summer tubes, wide mouthed and numerous. However, even in fall and winter some expanding growth goes on, although the tube mouths are very narrow and their number is small, making the wood appear solid. By starting at the center (pith) of a trunk and counting the concentric rings or bands of porous tube-ends, you have the age of the tree.

Good growing seasons produce wide bands of growth, dry or cool seasons produce narrower ones. Therefore, the bands are not of uniform width. You will see that in a tree's earlier years, all the bands were wider than they appear nearer to the outer bark, due to the vigorous expansion of youth. Careful studies made on very old trees—and upon fossil ones—have enabled scientists to assert some amazing things as to climatic conditions in ancient days. Correlating such data from all over the world has, furthermore, aided science to say a lot about long periods of drought and precipitation, and their effect upon our racial history. Great human migrations have been dated, and eras of luxuriant agriculture have been shown to be the cause of certain rich civilizations in the past. A count of the rings on some of the mammoth Sequoias of California proves them to be the oldest living things on earth: full-grown and aged when Christ was born.

Borrowing a Leaf from Nature

THERE are certain points where nature-study and science must meet face to face. Here is one. Unfortunately, it seems to be impossible to talk intimately about leaves without becoming either professorial or chatty. Even in a book like this, the chance of going to the first extreme is worth taking. It is hardly possible to borrow a leaf from Nature without borrowing some information from the library to go with it.

Despite the fairly general acceptance of the dictum: "In the Beginning was the Word"; so far as life-on-the-earth is concerned, it carries an obvious misprint. In the beginning—of all multicellular existence—was the Leaf.

Leaves, great and small, are able to perform a difficult chemical reaction, one which man in his laboratory has hardly been able to duplicate—and that only in part. In scientific phrase, green *chlorophyl* in leaf cells can split up the atmospheric compound known as carbon dioxide gas, and build its elements into a sugar. Then this chemical sugar is somehow changed into starch; and even into oils; and thus into plant food.—All animals live, directly or indirectly, on such plant starches, sugars and oils.

Innocent, dancing, simple-looking leaves of tree, grass and flowers,—these are actual food factories—the only *true* food factories on earth dealing with *true* "raw materials." Chlorophyl action, however, like the action of any other machinery, requires the application of power. That power is light. . . . Coal, wood, petroleum, natural gas, in fact, every fuel used by man, is transformed sunlight. But the green plant gets its fuel-power straight from the source of all energy on earth, the sun, then turns that energy into life-energy. No leaf, no life: not an exactly accurate aphorism (since chlorophyl resides in algæ, plant stems, etc., as well as in leaves) but a meaningful one.

No leaf, no life. If this profound fact were grasped, the doctrine of evolution would be inescapable. Animal life has only followed—like the parasitic phenomenon it is—where plant life has led it. Animal evolution, in a deep sense, is an ever-developing adaptation to the struggle for life made by vegetation everywhere. When the sea became crowded, green things went ashore; when the beach was overflowed by life, stemmed things crept further inland; when undergrowth became dense, trunks appeared. And animals pursued the plants—and each other.

Carnivorous animals who never eat vegetable food must get their nourishment from others who do. Even walrus, seal and whale, polar bear and deep-sea fishes, get their livelihood in this round-about way.

The leaf a factory? Yes, a factory æons before modern industrialism appeared in human affairs. Raw materials: water, carbon dioxide, soil miner-als. Machinery: the tiny grains of mysterious chlorophyl. Power: vibrating light. Process: breaking apart carbon and oxygen, and uniting them with water hydrogen to make a carbohydrate called sugar. . . . Here in simple epitome is the outline of nature's key and primary industry.

Up from the soil comes water (absorbed into the root-hairs by osmosis) holding in solution a dozen chemical salts; up it comes through the belt-line-conveyor of the sap-tubes in root and stem (pulled thus by capillarity) to the leaf-veins and spaces which are always evaporating excess water (transpiration) and so keeping the capillary flow going. Here, in sunlight striking through the outer skin of the leaf, takes place that mighty yet simple operation named "photosynthesis": food making by light.

Osmosis. Capillarity. Evaporation. Chlorophyl. Photosynthesis. Resounding words describing (not truly *explaining*) a patent process which is performed by a series of formulæ as secret as any possessed by human manufacturers. Studying these cumbersome words and trying to grasp their meaning is a nature-lover's duty—if he has any duty at all!

Wonder is all about us. Nothing in nature is more wonderful than anything else: that is the final conclusion to which all naturalists high and low eventually come. What a remarkable perfection of purpose; what an extraordinarily adjusted set of highly complex adaptations; in the meaning and activity of a leaf!

Yet . . . in the beginning—behind it all—there must have been something else, some Originator of chlorophyl. In the Beginning of the beginning was . . . well, let us say, God.

If you should be inclined to think the statement overdrawn that "this is truly the Age of Insects," you should study the summer leaves. During certain summers, and in some localities, you will be amazed to discover that, numberless as the leaves on the trees are, the insects which live among and upon them are yet more numerous. You will perhaps discover that *not one leaf* among all you look at but shows evidence of insect effects. Leaf-miners, gall flies, caterpillars, leaf-cutter bees, aphids, bettles—countless, unresting, eagerly hungry. What stirring drama is taking place in every tree, if we could but realize it!

Certain kinds of trees are more attacked than others—the Dogwood is fairly immune; but by August you will probably be unable to find anywhere a single tree or shrub the majority of whose leaves have not been mutilated. Then, if you reflect that fully half of the ravaging insects have parasites which prey upon them, and that in many cases these parasites are subject to parasites themselves, you reach a staggering conception of the phrase "the struggle for existence."

To go back for a moment to transpiration from leaves: it has been experimentally shown that a common grass plant evaporates from its leaves daily an amount of water *greater than its own weight*. One authority estimates that a large oak may evaporate annually into the air 226 times its weight of moisture! Rather more than 1,000 pounds of water is ordinarily transpired daily from a grass plot 25 x 100 feet! More drama, more wonder, more invisible expressions of mighty energy.

Handling such enormous amounts of soil-water,

it is not surprising that in a few months the veins of leaves become clogged by deposits of unusable chemical salt crystals and excretions. By the time autumn rolls around most leaves are so choked up that the presence of the deposits causes them to turn various colors. Soon after this the leaves die —and we have fall indeed. . . . Evergreens shed their leaves, too, but not all at one time as the deciduous trees do. Besides, the former's leaves do not get the sort of sap brought to them that the latter's do, and so their chemical impurities do not give the bright tints of autumn leaves.

Evaporation of excess water does not take place from all parts of a leaf, but only through tiny holes (called "stomata") on the under side. Not only does evaporation occur through them, but also the entrance of air which is another raw material going into the starch-making and growing process; so that if the stomata are clogged by dust and soot, a tree is literally both drowned and suffocated. Certain cities find it almost impossible to keep trees alive. (New York is one of them.) Poisonous fumes, as well as clogging dirt, kill a tree quickly through action by way of these breathing-holes. When a drought sets in, a leaf, as if realizing it ought to conserve its moisture, has the power to partly or wholly close its stomata.

Moreover, these holes open wider in cool weather and at night than in full heat of the sun.

So, all in all, a leaf appears to be a most remarkable piece of mechanism. But, as we have mentioned above, nothing is more wonderful than anything else.

Ways of Locating Birds' Nests

THE following suggestions are for beginning ornithologists well started along their pleasant way. In them are boiled down the experience of one whose thirty years at the game enable him occasionally to surprise his friends, and to wave a truly deprecatory hand when his success at locating birds' nests wins a bit of applause.—Who wouldn't have learned something after thirty years!

A few general remarks are set down first; followed by a discussion of eight types of approach to the art. For there are about this number of ways to go about it, depending on what you are looking for.

Why find nests?—It is rather useless to attempt answering such a question. If readers begin by putting this query, there is no need for them to read any further. If they don't know *why*, they are as yet not very deeply addicted to bird study. Nest finding is simply a cardinal part of bird study; even where photography is not to be the final purpose. One of the inherent peculiarities of human nature is that a definite and tangible *objective* adds zest to any business, art, sport or hobby. After all, there is no great need to record one's golf score or to keep track of the elusive count in tennis; for if these diversions are enjoyed solely for exercise and fun, the numerical result is theoretically unimportant. Yet we do get thrills from trying to win out over the game itself and our opponent. I am opposed to finding nests in order to collect birds' eggs, because I believe that no scientific end is to be attained any more from what used to be called "oology"; and because the resulting destruction of bird life is not justifiable—at least, for amateurs. But both a personal satisfaction and a possible addition to scientific knowledge do come from observing birds' home habits. A collection of nests *that have served their purpose* is, on the other hand, a harmless and delightful hobby.

Early morning is by far the best time to enjoy birds. Before eight A.M., whether in spring, summer or autumn, fall the hours that conform to their greatest activity. . . . Need I repeat that one's walk should always proceed in a general direction *away from* the sun? If your trip is an all-day affair, go west in the morning and east in the afternoon. It is impossible to distinguish colors when looking toward the sun, and the effects of solar glare blinds one's eyes to many other objects beside nests. When striving to identify a bird, always try to work around it to get the light at your back. And, as for identification, to be successful at all, you must use binoculars or field glasses. I have found powerful ones better than those moderately strong but featuring a wide field of vision. A good glass extends your range remarkably and allows you to watch a shy bird at a distance where eyesight would be useless. Not alone birds, but many a high-up nest can be discovered by using a glass, and furthermore, a study of one through it will often tell whether the nest is occupied or not and whether it is a last year's structure.

Of course it goes without saying that a successful technique of locating nests rests primarily on looking for *a particular nest*. Just going along searching for "a nest of some kind" is well-nigh useless. Once your attention has been attracted to a bird, and your suspicions definitely aroused, then follows the need that you be fairly well grounded in two facts: one, that the time of year is likely to involve the nesting time of the species; and two, that the situation or location of this particular species' homestead points to a well-defined place to look. You'll not be trying to discover a Wood Thrush's nest on the ground or a Wilson Thrush's

(Veery's) in a sapling. Nor will you be expecting Goldfinches to be building before July 1st. These bits of knowledge are presupposed; they can be gleaned from books. A certain percentage of your finds will be just plain accidents, no matter how expert you may become; but a deep-dyed enthusiast does not get as much glee from these accidental windfalls as from a treasure he has put all his knack and understanding into.

Speaking generally, the more ground you cover in a season, the more nests you will locate. I am aware that there are two schools of contenders on this point: some holding that a relatively small area intensively "cultivated" will yield more than a great deal of necessarily casual walking done per acre. But I incline to the latter theory—except as regards certain areas especially rich in avian life.

There is yet another trick of observation to be acquired. Not every feathered biped which you flush from some tangle or otherwise promising spot, even if it starts up with considerable protesting noise, is anxious about a nearby nest. Particularly when a parent is leading about a litter of half-grown young, its actions and notes may deceive the best of us. A bird close to its nest is likely to go through a very well-established set of actions. The chirpings of anxiety, the flitting from place to place, the repeated efforts to get a good sight of you, are carried out by a nesting bird to much greater length and persistency, than those of a suddenly surprised feeding or roosting individual who has no home-ties connecting it with the vicinity. Only experience will enable a person to judge—and even then, not infrequently is he deceived. Then again, certain species, especially if their eggs are newly laid or the clutch is incompleted, will either slink away from the neighborhood completely or will endeavor to lead you away by making a fuss in the distance. You just have to *learn* the reaction-patterns of each species.

Although the following hints may be counsels of perfection and may not actually admit of being communicated to others, I am bound to urge all bird students to try to develop "the listening ear and the seeing eye." An old hand at ornithology, no matter where he is or what he may be doing, will stop short and note any unusual bird sound. Any flutter or flash or flight, not automatically accounted for by him, will bring his attention to instant focus. This habit is the one I refer to. I suppose it only comes through practice and a very keen interest in the subject. Many a hint as to nests or rare visitors around the home; or for that matter anywhere along the countryside walk; comes from a single squawk or call-note or from an un-repeated glimpse of a strange manner of flight. To become adept at nest-finding one has to call upon all his assets, accidental as well as premeditated. Unless one cannot immediately account for everything he hears or sees as it slips past him, he should learn to stop and take further bearings. Persistency will usually net him further rewards.

Sometimes I am inclined to believe there is such a thing as a "sixth sense" developed in the experienced ornithologist. He will again and again seem instinctively *to know* just where a nest ought to be—and he goes there and sees it. I remember a few striking instances. I had never been able to discover the nest of a Northern Water-thrush. For years, up and down two brooks with which I was very familiar, I had gone carefully searching, too minutely, I fear, and not giving time enough for quiet observation. Then, last summer, as I was mowing the lawn, a certain Water-thrush song, out of the thousands which they had sung since arrival, stopped me. I left the lawn-mower in the furrow, as Israel Putnam did the plow, and walked straight down the stone steps to the brook, crossed it, went a hundred feet down to the over-turned roots of a big beech, and laid my hands directly on—my first nest! I cannot recall any reasoning process during the incident. A similar occurrence with a Worm-eating Warbler: Like the half-wit boy who managed to bring home the lost horse—I can say: "I went there and he had." Or, rather *she* had hidden that rare nest of hers exactly where I went to look for it. That it takes half-witted persons, who can "think what they'd do if they were a horse" (or a Warbler), to put themselves exactly into an animal's frame of mind, I cannot admit. . . . Another memorable March morning several years ago, I awoke to hear a far-away boisterous racket of some crows. At that moment, I simply *felt sure* I could find a Great Horned Owl's nest over there—and after four miles of walking straight to the spot, I did. The crows had given the necessary hint.

Under eight headings I have classified some ideas which may enable you to be a little more successful than you were last season.

Imitating the Cowbird

"Set a thief to catch a thief" is certainly good tactics. Set a bird to catch a bird's nest is the best of schemes. How is it that Madame Cowbird, she who is shockingly polyandrous and makes no nest of her own—in both these respects unique among North American birds—manages to locate the residences of so many small feathered sisters and bring them so much trouble? She lays her eggs in with the clutches of perhaps thirty species. No one knows how many eggs she will thus deposit in a season—perhaps ten or a dozen, to judge by her more orthodox relatives. How does she find so many places to lay them? Rarely, if ever, will she be unwise enough to pick out a nest whose eggs are well started in incubation; for that would bring her offspring into life small and helpless in the midst of the legitimate brood. How does she judge their stage of incubation? She doesn't judge, and can't. She watches and watches, slyly perching in some likely spot, until she sees a bird carrying nesting material or going to the secret spot to lay. Then she flies down, drives off the protesting parents, and leaves her own evil time-bomb. In due course the "bomb" goes off and the highly active and querulous young Cowbird hatches in the alien nest, from that time on to crowd aside the rest of the nestlings and secure the lion's share of the food. Often Mother Cowbird (a most "unnatural" mother! gets her egg into a nest before there are any others laid; in which event it may happen that the owners simply desert the premises, or, cleverly enough, construct a whole new floor right on top of the thing, and continue their incubation above it. Plenty of trouble she does bring to every family on which she encroaches; frequently the other young are starved to death or are pushed from the nest; and after the group have left the place, the fledgling Cowbird so dogs and pesters its foster-mother that the rest of them get quite neglected. (Incidentally, it is worth noting that the female Cowbird can *control* her laying intervals more adeptly than other birds.)

Imitate her methods, clandestine as they may be. Watchful waiting—the endless patience and time consumed being of no account—will no doubt enable you to locate as many bird homes as she. Passive persistence, one might call this method. In a modified way, it can be applied wherever you have strong reason to think a much-desired nest is nearby. Of course, few of us can afford the time required—what's a Cowbird's time worth compared with ours? But it gets results. I have time and again found Cowbird's eggs in such wholly concealed nests that I marveled at her skill. Almost every species, from Chipping Sparrow size to that of Robin and Towhee, has to face this minor calamity. And, so far as I have observed, the foster parents never shirk their duty towards the foundling.

Holes in Trees

Everywhere and always, even in autumn and winter, it should be an invariable rule to knock violently with a stick upon every dead stump that has a hole in it. Who knows what may be hidden inside? On occasions I have had whole families of Flying Squirrels emerge in a hurry; once eight came out and floated swiftly away to the four compass points. Red Squirrels also may appear. As for nesting birds, nearly without exception the sitter will fly out and inform you of what is within. Screech Owls may be using a den, with an entrance surprisingly small, as a daylight roosting place; but they will not come forth unless you drag them out by hand. All the Woodpeckers and Sapsuckers housekeep in holes; then there are Wrens, Creepers, Nuthatches, Screech Owls, Crested Flycatchers, Titmice, Prothonotary Warblers, Bluebirds and Sparrow Hawks to expect. Such nests are of little use for observation, even assuming you may reach them. But if you really want to look inside, here is a suggestion: With a cut-off and very sharp key-hole saw, cut—on a bevel—a section from the wood down as far as necessary, and, putting a finger in the hole, break out the section towards you. Later it can be replaced by fitting it back and driving in four or five thin finishing-nails. Almost never will a bird desert after such an operation—unless perhaps when the eggs are entirely fresh. If you intend doing much tree climbing, you should equip yourself with climbing irons like a linesman's. None but the biggest of trees or the rottenest can defy you then. In any case, don't fail to rap on every dead tree with a good sound stick lying near.

The Checkerboard Plan

Suppose you have located a definite area—say two acres or less—in which you surmise there is something worth finding. Plot out that area and walk slowly back and forth in paths ten feet apart, first having conspicuously marked the two ends of your first line with your hat, handkerchief or scarf. Conscientiously done, there is small likelihood of anything escaping you. This technique is especially suited to discovering nests in brier patches, tall grass, open pastures, or upland fields where you are seeking Killdeer and Bartramian Sandpiper nests. Strange as it seemed to me at the time, I once had to *complete* the checkerboard, in all four directions, before I at length stumbled upon a most cunningly concealed Marsh Hawk's eyrie amid a sea of blueberry bushes.

In the Marshes

It is useless to work here unless you wear hip-high wading boots. If the jungle is dense, you will have to make your up-and-down, criss-crossing lines very close together. Two things need to be remembered in exploring marshes: more totally unexpected birds will be likely to be there than in any other area; and a majority of the sitters are not close sitters, but will have slid quietly away before you come anywhere near. What with Ducks, Rails, Bitterns, Marsh Wrens, Swamp Sparrows, Blackbirds, Gallinules and Marsh Hawks, a marsh is a far more enticing place to inspect than a beginner is apt to imagine. I recommend, for many and varied thrills, a big marsh on a June day over any other natural bird preserve in the country. Two mishaps have to be guarded against here: that you do not overbalance on a tussock or Muskrat lodge and go sprawling into the unsavory water; and that a vicious and over-sized Snapping Turtle doesn't take a bite at your boot-tip. Go slowly, feeling your footing ahead with your toe, and you are not likely to sink suddenly in over the tops of your boots.

The Meadow Grass

Chiefly to find where Bobolinks, Quail, Grass-hopper Sparrows and Meadowlarks have nested, get a friend to go along and take with you a hundred feet of clothesline. Drag the rope between you; and ten to one, out will pop your sitting birds directly from their eggs. Without such a scheme one may waste hours vainly trying to find them, for the birds usually run through the grass some distance before they fly up. Even watching the owners until they alight into the wide expanse is often bootless, because they commonly dive into it many feet from their home site.

For Hawks and Owls

March, April and early May, before leaves come out, are the days for this strenuous branch of the service. Steel climbers, of course. . . . It's *miles* here that count; you have to tramp the thick woodlands for hours, pounding upon the trunks of every tree which holds a possible occupied nest. Most species of Raptores, as well as the common crow, settle in second-hand eyries as often as new ones, and only the sharp use of a glass and plenty of muscle in your trunk-rapping will tell which are the "live" piles of sticks and which only stark

platforms or squirrel caches. When you are puzzled, you must sit concealed near by and await the
return of the native—if he or she does come—or
else subject yourself to a vigorous climb for
nothing.

Shade-Tree Nests

Into this category falls the hardest of all nests
to locate. In the first place, there are so many
shade trees and so few nests per tree. Secondly,
heavy leafage is baffling, mainly because leaves
usually are set at right angles to the sun's rays and
form a kind of covering shingle roof from below
as well as from above. But if one *takes time
enough* with each suspected tree, he can be fairly
well assured of results. Circle the tree, and let
your glance run out from the trunk along every
limb to its tip. If it is Hummingbirds' nests you
covet, travel along the outer edge of your woods
or along the water-courses or gullies which run
through it. Only the *branch-ends* need be studied
for these treasures; and, likely enough, the mother
Hummer will squeak and buzz at you as soon as
you approach very near. An old orchard is apt to
hold an uncommon number of residents; not only
Hummingbirds (I believe about one old orchard
in three is sure to harbor a pair); but many other

species. An orchard is so easy to search thoroughly that nothing should go unfound if one but put his heart into the task. Never pass up a chance to census an old-fashioned apple orchard!

Some Special Cases

There are several "special cases" which I have not space enough to discuss here. I merely list them, and advise you to go to two or three standard bird books for the information which will make their discovery an outstanding delight. These are difficult to find; but having found them, you will be well pleased: Northern Water-thrush, Killdeer, Over-bird, Whip-poor-will, Nighthawk, Woodcock, Short-eared Owl, both Kinglets, Ruffed Grouse and White-breasted Nuthatch.

The sport of bird study is enormously enhanced by using the camera. Once having found your bird and its nest, the use of concealing "blinds" demands all your native ingenuity. But nest photographing can be done to an amazing detail. In concluding just here, I urge you to read a few of the several splendid books on this pursuit, and really in earnest try out your luck at it!

Snow and Eggs

I THINK it is not generally realized, even by those who have made bird study an active hobby, how early some birds start to lay eggs. The few instances below of snow-covered nests which have come under my personal observation may be put completely in the shade by Canadian records; but for New York State the species mentioned may be fairly representative of the total probabilities likely to be encountered. North of the line of the Old Mohawk Trail (now the Erie Canal) snows frequently descend up until May 15th—by May 1st practically all species of *raptores* have decided upon their nesting sites and over two-thirds of them have commenced incubation. Therefore, to the notes following may readily be added in theory nearly every hawk or owl we have.

In 1906 I found a typical nest of the White-rumped Shrike in a thorn-apple bush. On April 9th, when the set of six eggs was completed, a light fall of snow the night previous cozily cottoned them in so that only a bit of each shell was visible. The parents were anxiously about, but the mother did not attempt to sit all that day. Three days later, she was observed brooding her charges as though nothing had interrupted. All the eggs hatched in due course—a result impossible had the eggs actually frozen.

A Great-Horned Owl's eyrie, to which I most laboriously climbed several Februaries ago, had its two white billiard-ball eggs resting upon a floor of ice which had formed beneath the sitting bird's body. A night or so of below-zero weather is usual during the incubation period of this owl; sleet storms and heavy falls of snow are common occurrences; for it is the earliest breeder north of the Gulf States. It is a mystery how their eggs are prevented from freezing. The supposition naturally is that from the moment of laying they are not deserted a moment, a guess substantiated by the fact that both sexes incubate by turns.

The first Woodcock's nest I ever discovered was mantled with a thin feathering of March snow. Only two of the final clutch of four eggs had then been laid. As this plover of the woods and pastures nests often in mid-March, the mother's back must often be whitened. As a rule, Woodcocks are second only to the Great-Horned Owl, as early nesters.

One April day within my memory, a hole in a

tall fence post, which chanced to face northwestward, came in for a generous filling of snow. I knew that a pair of Bluebirds already had chosen this place, so I investigated. Sure enough, the pale blue jewels were in there completely buried, for the cavity was half full. The parents left in despair, for it was several days before the weather moderated sufficiently to melt the snow inside the post.

Twice I have climbed to Red-shouldered Hawk's platforms after April blizzards, to find the nests fringed with snow, but the eggs, sheltered by the sitting parent, were warm and dry. On April 16, 1913, however, a domicile in a small beech, which held one handsome egg, had received no such protection from the quick change in the weather, and it was as cold an object as one would expect to dig out of an inch of preserving snow. I have found it to be a well established Red-shoulder trait to sit the nest very closely and bravely during damp drizzly days; while on warm ones, they will much more readily fly off when the tree trunk is struck. Until the full set is laid, they appear to have only a casual regard for the fractional part—hence the snow and rain which they allow to descend on partial clutches: a somewhat common thing to discover.

What I regard as an all-time record for northern New York is the finding of a Prairie Horned Lark's nest holding four eggs on March 29th. Although the nest site (on the ground in a pasture) was fairly dry, remnants of disappearing snowdrifts lay all around and pasture hollows were full of slushy ice! This may be a common surrounding for Alaska or Athabasca birds, but I doubt if any other bird in the United States ever builds next door to melting drifts—surely not outside the Rocky Mountains.

Part Three

GOSSIP AROUND THE FIREPLACE

Done for the day and the year with the sights and sounds afield and afoot, we now gather around the winter fire; a place to trade experiences and tell tales. From dissertating miscellaneously upon "how to do it," we pass on here to the relaxation of reporting and recounting. As elders are wont, in the chimney-corner we wax reminiscent, shake heads over old days, plan plans for new days. . . . A blessed thing that every twelvemonth Nature runs again over her cycle, and the old is ever new; dreams put aside, whose fruition has been postponed for this cause and that, reawaken old desires, galvanize old resolves. What's a fireplace for on a winter night!

But—one moment!—an urgent message must first be delivered.

From Country Homes to Black Bears

Own Two Homes!

PLAN plans? Dream dreams?—Who of the town has not longed for a retreat in the country; a removed, quiet, nestling bit of a shelter of one's own as an escape from workaday routine? Most modest, perhaps,—the more modest the easier had!

I am moved to exhort my readers on how readily such a roof-and-bed may be acquired by most of them today. I wonder if you families out there in a busier and more crowded world than mine realize how simple (simple as things go in our complex and hasty lives) is the attainment of such a wish.

'Tis only inertia's north wind that blows nobody good. The blizzard of economic change which has been steadily sweeping over the rural East for the past thirty years has untenanted many a farm. Countless pastures and meadowlands, cleared by the toil of our forefathers, not only are reverting to the County Tax Collector, ex officio, but are at the same time being reclaimed by Nature's insatiable green "squatters." One hundred and fifty thousand four hundred and sixty-six farms ceased to exist as farms during the period 1920-1930; over nineteen million acres went out of cultivation, and somewhat over four million countryfolk stopped being farmers! Over these hard-won clearings once wrested from the woods is spreading The New Wilderness.

The farm houses stand empty! Probably not one eastern farm in ten *pays*. That is, truly pays in the long run, from its *production* and not its capital value. Properly allowing for thorough upkeep and for a decent money wage for its owner, few eastern farms can be called prosperous. Speaking by and large, when the "old folks" pass on to more celestial acres, there are no sons and daughters to carry on; and new farmers will not come to such homesteads, because there is no new crop of farmers. Farms put on the market stay there, and stay and stay. The foregoing is but a commonplace summing-up—no news to the rural population out our way: and I have seen parallel conditions all through New England, New Jersey and Pennsylvania.

Such a blizzard, I say, is a warm zephyr of good luck to townsfolk. Run-down farms, in all stages of agricultural flabbiness, can today be bought for a song. "No reasonable offer refused" is the pathetic cry from every dirtroad byway—and "reasonable" is an elastic adjective.

Let not your conscience trouble you, O reacherout after country air and Nature's gifts, that such acreages "cost more to put up and keep in shape" than to buy. Let the fences go, and the meadows and pastures sprout haw bushes, briers, smilax and white birches. What matter?—they will do so anyway, whether *you* buy them or not.

If there is not a house on the place, build a little one. Not much money is needed for the venture, if the cottage is not of winter-proof construction. Week-ends, summers, autumn and winter holidays—even Christmas and New Year's—it will welcome you and you it. One absolutely needs but a bed or two, a few elderly chairs and tables, a kerosene range, oil lamps, and, of course, a spring, well, or brook for water. From such enforced simplicity up, up to the rich obesity of a country estate and a house with all modern improvements, is a range of costs likely to hit most fairly prosperous families.

I beseech you: look around about your town or city. Be not content with the husks of life the city gives you to eat! Enter your car and set out prospecting along country roads. You will not have burned a gallon of gasoline ere some such old place as I have described appears alongside and begs to change ownership. I know of ten within walking distance of my own refuge any one of which for years could have been yours, with all its acreage, for a price below what the buildings would cost to replace: some indeed for less than the price of a fancy automobile. And this situation is not confined to our township, by any means.

I can conceive of no investment more likely to yield more enduring happiness, more recreation and health, and more outlets for that hobby-urge within us all, than buying a second home. Be it ever so humble, there's no place like home number two. . . .

These few words to the wise are sufficient. From a nature-lover's heart this suggestion comes with a double force; from the lips of one who has "gone and done likewise," it emerges with the twofold assurance born of experience and self-congratulation.

Having boldly disposed of this momentous question in so summary a fashion, we must get along to other and less human matters. At first thought, it may seem a very far cry indeed to proceed from a home in the country to such topics as earthworms, rabbits, mice and bears. Yet, in strict truth, acquaintance and adventures with the latter are very likely to follow from life in the former, in reality as they do here in these pages. This I can assert from my own encounters inasmuch as on my country acres I have met them all except bruin, —not to mention tenants so captivating as deer, skunks, woodchucks, grouse, muskrats, snakes, turtles, birds, insects, flowers, too numerous to catalogue.

Of the Earth, Earthy

If it was Evolution which put earthworms *in* the map, it was certainly the illustrious Darwin who put them *on* the map—for it was he who publicized their absolute necessity to mankind. "Agriculture [as practiced in 1850] could not exist [he proved] without them." Both by leavening the soil from its natural hard solidity, and by admitting air and water to the roots of vegetation, they make possible crops and plant life as we know them. Darwin stated that in England's garden soil at least 50,000 worms per acre existed, and eighteen tons of earth per acre were yearly "eaten" by them!

Limbricus terrestris is a two-sexed animal. Quite

sufficient unto itself, and quite too occupied to bother about courtship, it maintains itself by a strange process of hermaphroditism. However, its eggs do not develop into young through asexual (parthenogenetic) reproduction such, for instance, as is the case with aphids and daphnia during summer months; but one end of the worm is male, the other female. Eggs are fertilized by male germs —not, surprisingly enough, by germs of the worm which produces the eggs, but by those of another worm which has filled the first one's seminal receptacles. At the same time its own receptacles are filled, a worm is impregnating the other's receptacles likewise. So cross-fertilization seems to be invariably accomplished.

Every adult worm you examine has a whitish thickened ring near one end. This ring secretes a circle of tough membrane in the spring, which by action of tiny bristles along its sides, it works forward along its body. As the hardening ring of membrane passes over the ovary's openings, eggs are squeezed into it and, as it passes on further forward and over the receptacle's orifices, sperms are squeezed into it. The worm slips backward out of the ring, which then elastically closes at both ends forming a capsule wherein fertilization and hatching occur. Emerging, the minute youngsters shift for themselves—that is, they begin swallowing earth on their own account.

Out of the engulfed earth, limbricus absorbs its nourishment. Having no eyes, it can easily be shown to be affected by light; and, having no brain, it is known to possess two or three tricks for ascertaining danger and either remaining quiet in its presence, or slipping swiftly back into its burrow. For it has a private burrow, and does not usually try to dig itself in at random when alarmed, unless it has strayed too far from home.

Try the Robin's habit of pulling an earthworm from its burrow, and unless you do precisely as the Robin does, you will usually break it in two. The bird, you may have observed, pulls steadily and not with a jerk. The muscles of the worm, which have contracted and forced the four rows of tiny bristles into the wall of the burrow, soon become exhausted; then it cannot but slip out as it is pulled.

Earthworms are *segmented* worms, made up in sections,—did you ever notice that? It may have as many as twenty segments. If broken apart, it has the ability to re-form itself. No one need feel sorry when he cuts an earthworm in two while digging. It's all in a lifetime; and in a few weeks the animal is itself once more. Strictly speaking it can be classed as a nocturnal animal, for most of its moving and eating—at any rate, above ground—is done in the dark. As it is not inclined to hurry in at dawn, "the early bird catches the worm." Worm-casts, those little pellets of coiled earth on paths and golfing greens, are formed by the expelled intestinal contents, which it can only discharge above the surface without blocking up its beloved burrow.

There is considerable lore about earthworm life besides the things I have mentioned; but as no creature is easier to study, you can find most of it out yourself.

First, Know Your Rabbit

The quaint direction, in the old recipe book on preparing rabbit stew, to "First, catch your rabbit," is equally good advice for the beginning naturalist. Catching him, however, is as well done by the eye as the trap, for the latter's purpose. All over the eastern states, the Cottontail bunny is one of the commonest truly wild animals and one of the easiest to practice on.

Entirely contrary to the folklore and song of our land, the "rabbit hole" is a rarity. In some sections it is nonexistent. When bunny takes occasional refuge in a burrow, it is not one of its own digging. Evolution's lesson has compelled the tribe to avoid holes. The woodchuck is a savage inmate for an intruder to face underground; skunks are quite as bad for another reason; but the American Hare (alias the Cottontail) has only its legs for defense, and when it enters a hole it literally puts *both* feet in the grave. Weasels would wipe out all hole-haunting rabbits in a few years because the former would probably increase rapidly with such prey available. So our Hare—unlike the Rabbit of Europe—spends summer and winter alike where there is plenty of rear-elbow room.

Is a Hare a stupid little animal? Personally, I change my mind on this question every few months. Sometimes it seems to exhibit great craft in eluding dogs; then, again, its overreliance upon sitting still and being unnoticed makes it easy pickings for sharp-nosed dogs and foxes—not to mention hunters with guns. I have seen the young ones frisk, roll, dart and play for half-hours on end; but believe that after attaining full size they are lazy and sluggish, except, of course, when actually pursued. And I think there is a reason for such slowing-up. Parasites. Our bunnies are well-known to be infested with intestinal and even muscular parasite worms, which, like the effects of human hookworm and swine trichinosis, dulls their vitality. Bunny is not the only wild animal so afflicted—nearly all the rodent family suffer. The woodchuck, wood rat, white-foot mouse, bat, mole, and other creatures, will usually be found swarming with blood-sucking fleas. An astonishing find of a litter of half-grown red squirrels *on October 1, 1930,* impressed me for another reason beside their freakish unseasonableness. Although born in an apple tree where the presence of fleas would be hard to account for, the seven of them, huddled in a snug limb hollow, were alive with these insects. At least fifty inhabited each youngster! . . . Hares carry fleas also, along with their other curses. Perhaps such unhealthiness accounts for their occasional listlessness.

Usually three litters are born to a mother Cottontail every year. Only through the aid of your dog's nose or by sheer accident, will you discover the "nest," for it is hidden in a shallow scooped-out depression among grass tussocks. Above it, when she leaves, mother Hare carefully composes the dry grass and litter so that human eyes cannot detect it at all. She lines it thickly with fur from her underparts, but never a wisp will show outside. The hollow is not large enough for her to creep into; in nursing her babies she simply lies down close beside the spot and pushes aside the covering so they may reach her. I partly uncovered a litter in my backyard this summer two evenings in succession, but each morning following, the mother had replaced the materials and made the spot as undetectable as before. Moreover, the fur which I had purposely left strewn around in sight was gathered up entirely and put back—to the very last hair—and nothing appeared to reveal the nest. On my third interference, she moved the young ones to another spot, and I did not see them until they were shifting for themselves about the place. Wandering cats, dogs, foxes, skunks, owls, hawks, snakes, and even crows, take such toll of the little rabbits that probably not one in a dozen reach breeding maturity.

From about latitude 42 degrees northward, the Varying Hare appears, and gets gradually more common as the Canadian line is reached, where it is far commoner than the Cottontail. This larger Hare changes its brown coat for a white one— completely so in the New England highlands, and partly so south of them. As so many naturalists have observed, this Hare (called also Snowshoe Rabbit because of its back feet) comes and goes at irregular intervals, so that some winters few will be seen where once they were somewhat abundant.

A prettier sight than a crouching snow-white rabbit beneath the evergreens is hard to imagine. I couldn't shoot one and call it sport any more than I could shoot my dog!

Because it is prolific, despite its many enemies, the Cottontail Hare can maintain its race nearly everywhere, especially in the neighborhood of suburban homes and farm houses. Although you may be unaware of the presence of even one from March to October, the snow will tell its tale and show you just how several of them can carry on outside when you are dependent upon your roofs, walls, and fires for existence. Hard to inveigle into a box-trap when green food is plenty everywhere; in fall and winter, a carrot or turnip bait enables you to catch them almost at will. Unlike a Red Squirrel, a Cottontail readily tames, and loses both its fear of you and its resentment of handling. But guard your tulips and narcissus in early spring when succulent green is scarce! Every one of my bulb shoots was nibbled to the ground last March by the half-dozen unpaying guests which tenanted my place undisturbed. I had to use wire fenders in order that the bulbs might rejuvenate themselves and come to blossom.

White-foot, the Outdoor Mouse

White-foot is not the only outdoor mouse, of course. And not *always* outdoors, alas! At times it presumes to dwell in the same house with you and use the same cellar. Not that I mind that; Brown Bats, Mole-shrews, Norway Rats and Flying Squirrels have done the same thing. But I believe I am correct in saying that White-foot is the only mouse hereabout who commonly disputes the best indoor nooks with the immigrant House Mouse. And my traps at home have caught about as many of the one as the other. That is why I am sorry he comes inside. . . . I have enjoyed so many interesting contacts with "the outdoor mouse" that I am particularly fond of the breed.

There is no difficulty in distinguishing the two species; White-foot is altogether a rustic, outdoor-looking sort of mouse; large-eyed, big-eared, thick-furred, plump and slow-moving. Its underparts are all white—very clean and white. Its back is a lighter shade than either the House or the Field Mouse, sometimes showing glints of gold on it.

So commonly does it put up for the autumn (and even for the winter, in this region) in abandoned Towhee, Wood Thrush and Song Sparrow nests, that, after the leaves have fallen, investigation of all such nests is a good way of discovering one. As a rule, only a single rodent occupies such a structure, which it has domed and thatched with barkstrips and grass, rarely storing any food in it. Its larder is elsewhere close by. Disturb the nest, and out creeps the inmate reluctantly and makes off to some better concealment. Come back in an hour, and the chances are—if the day is chill— that it has returned first. In my garage and in the henhouse beneath the feed barrel or under the floor litter, there are invariably one or two nests at any season. There the domicile is a ball of dry grass or a bunch of any other handy material. Around the premises elsewhere, a tree hollow, a Chipmunk hole or a brier tangle suffices.

White-foot shows little fear, especially when it has young, at which time it deserts them only as a last resort to save itself. Often, as the mother escapes, she carries one or two clinging to her teats. . . . What I particularly want to hear from one —but never have—is the musical twitter or chirp which certain observers say it utters. I have never heard even a squeak from one. . . . Also, I do not understand why it is called Deer Mouse in some localities. Squirrel Mouse would be more appropriate, because it does resemble somewhat a flying squirrel, and many of its actions are curiously squirrel-like. Like this squirrel and all mice, it is mainly nocturnal and does not hibernate.

My efforts at taming separate individuals have met with poor success. I don't know just why. Other mice frequently die overnight from nothing but fright when imprisoned in a cage, and so do young rabbits and squirrels. This is not so surprising. These are very timorous creatures. It may be that White-foot's comparative sluggishness conceals an equal inward upset, even though it is not apparent. But, put a mother and her babies together in a quiet cage, and they all soon become tame and can be readily handled. I doubt not, however, but that such holds true for any other mouse species; I have not experimented much with others.

As Thoreau pointed out, the reason why mankind suffer from winter cold is that they inhabit houses big enough to store a huge amount of furniture and other gear. By using a long narrow box, he said, a reasonable amount of lining would obviate coal bills and heating plants, with all the personal drudgery required to pay for them. Now, here is just where so many of the wild creatures score. White-foot, for example, minds the winter not at all, for after his daily bit of food hunting and zestful sport in the snow, he merely crawls into a snug bed which he exactly fits and is as warm as fresh toast. Under and over the snow are his runways and tracks, but deeply tucked away in stump or burrow will be his home.

Teddy Bears and Others

If we think of puppies, kittens and hares as totally helpless when born and for some weeks afterward, what word shall we apply to new-born Opossums and Black Bears? In two quite unrelated animal orders, the Marsupials and the Plantigrades respectively, occurs the birth of young not only in a helpless state, but in what must be regarded as a *premature* state.

'Possums when no larger than beans actually leave the mother's uterus in a semi-embryonic condition, having had but thirteen days within! They seem to possess but two faculties at that time: the ability to crawl (as they do, feebly, up into the maternal pouch on the outside of the abdomen) and, thereafter, the ability to seize and hang on to a milk-giving teat there for a period of six weeks. Among all the wonders of adaptation to which evolution has given rise, none is more astonishing than this.* The more so, perhaps, when it is realized that a litter of 'Possums frequently number from fifteen to eighteen—probably the largest litter among North American mammals!

This curious trait of premature birth, which in their case has enabled the Marsupials to produce more young than they could carry within the body and yet escape enemies and hunt food, has analogy in the Plantigrades; though with the latter the peculiarity works to a different end than large families. The clan of the bear "that *walks* like a man" has few young at a birth. Bears hibernate and remain foodless for months. It is not at all clear just why it is more in line with their vital economy that, during this fasting period, the twins, or triplets, should be suckled instead of developed within a placenta; but the babies are born early, when no larger than a man's fist, and are breast-fed. Madame Bruin has a pair of thoracic breasts, by the way, and not an udder or rows of abdominal teats as have all other quadrupeds except elephants, and this fact works to the mother's advantage in protecting them.

Many northern animals do carry their young-

* For a thrilling account of the birth and development of 'Possums, see Mr. Carl G. Hartman's article in *Nature Magazine* for August, 1930.

sters through the winter, to give them birth in spring—but bears, arctic and temperate, must be ready, it would appear, to go forth and battle for sustenance at the first break of spring. As hibernators, they must stir out as early as possible to begin the stern struggle to fill up. Often they must travel far and wide, and travel light; so that weight and agility are great assets. This, I suppose, is partly why the helpless bearlets are snuggled into the mother's warm fur in the den for the first month of their lives. Mother stays away from the den, at first, no longer than necessary. When her cubs are able to toddle along with her, they would be easy prey to wolves, lynxes and wild cats, but that she can sweep them securely in between her flat belly and firmly planted shanks, and use her paws to fend off attack. After they grow too large for this, the mother spanks them up a tree and prepares for defense below. The "manly art of self-defense" is even more essential for a bear than a boy to master, and its lessons begin early in childhood.

When I was a boy Black Bear cubs came into our possession nearly every spring. Backwoodsmen for miles around would bring them in. Our store windows became the accepted spot to which all the captured infant bruins of the countryside came for display and sale, though we rarely had more than four at a time. Indeed, I doubt whether more than that number could be herded together in any one place, other than a jail cell, without far-reaching consequences. When the youngsters reached us, they were commonly from ten to four-teen weeks old; but born so notoriously tiny and underdeveloped, this age found them at just the liveliness of a month-old kitten.

Unquestionably these fuzzy brownish-black cubs were the drollest of all God's creatures, ex-cepting none. For five minutes at a stretch, as if by rounds, a pair would stand and face each other in a give-and-take encounter which sent us into convulsions. How they acquire so young such real ability at feinting, dodging, sidestepping, ducking and clinching, is a marvel. They possess at that age a muscular coordination much superior to a young kitten. Lacking the lightning but random quick-ness of some animals, their movements had all the more appearance of calculated and intelligent di-rection. Sometimes three or four of the fat little rascals would roll in one wildly clawing, biting mass, tiny squeaks and squeals emanating now and then, as an unusually liberal nip of an ear or over-enthusiastic tweak of a tail carried over from frolic into spite. Climbing everywhere and up anything, was a favorite amusement, a mien of pseudo-gravity always enveloping them during any of their unaccompanied adventures. Their round heads, sparkling beady eyes, and sensitive black muzzles, surmounted by two perky, wide-flaring ears clothed in velvet fur, made a cartoon of mirth. Even in inactivity you found them irresistible. Sleeping, they won your heart by their chubby helplessness.

During regulation, four-square, frozen-in, Adirondack winters, our cubs (generally as twins) were born, often in ice caves that only late March suns could unlock. The hibernating mother's breath has made the snow walls of her den an armor of ice so thick that she cannot break out until spring. Meantime, sightless and furless for nearly four weeks, the cubs hardly try to move. They make up for it completely, though, when once they do get started.

Next to dogs, I suppose the word omnivorous applies more accurately to a bear than to any other animal. Our bears, true to ancestral taste, cared more for a lump of sugar or a spoonful of honey than for better approved and more temperate dietary.

About the time their nips began to be skin-puncturing matters, father would have us crate and ship them to a New Jersey game dealer, who in turn sold them to the zoos and circuses of the world. This part of the procedure was poignant to us. Surely nothing we boys ever got out of the twenty-five dollars paid to father was half so much fun as the article he sold!

When Teddy Bears first came in, their magic talisman of success was thought to lie in their first name; but long-continued and undiminished popularity is convincing proof that the last name held the secret. They are bear cubs: that is sufficient to win childish approval the world over. For, by now, they are not an American fad; they belong to all lands and peoples—perhaps to the ages. London and Paris shops stock them; you will see them in Sydney and Auckland; Japanese workmen are manufacturing them; Cairo has them for sale; Hong Kong's merchants will display them to you; the Italian boys and girls own them; Buenos Aires department stores would not be without them; in India you may sometimes see a "ryot" waif hugging one to its brown bosom. It's the bear, not the "teddy" that has conquered the juvenile world. As further proof, just witness the fact that recent best sellers each for two successive years, were books intimately revolving around "Winnie the Pooh!"

Hummingbird Traits

I HAVE always loved Hummingbirds. They tell me that once when I was a tiny youngster in a baby carriage, a Hummer came and stole nectar from a bouquet of flowers lying upon my coverlet. Perhaps my interest started there.

Later, when I began to take notice of things ornithological and had started in an awkward boyish hand a list of "Birds I Have Learned," there was provided by happy chance an unusual opportunity to observe the sprightly little mites right in my dooryard. An old buckeye horse-chestnut tree stood in our grounds, surrounded by giant sugar maples. For years it was a regular rendezvous for Hummers on their northward migrations. The tree blossomed from top to bottom just about the time when the migration journeys were on, and every morning for a week in early May, at least a dozen breakfasted there together en route. The long, upstanding pinnacles of sweet flowers with which the tree was decorated attracted astonishing numbers. In the course of two hours I have counted thirty-six visitors. Squeaking and buzzing

—now and then with that bass, cutting buzz, which makes you think them angry or spiteful— they pursued one another about the tree and among the maples, between times when they fed daintily from the airy plumes. I soon discovered that these early arrivals were always males; they seemed to precede the females by a week or ten days. It is an unforgettable memory: those iridescent backs and shoulders, those jet-black heads, those eye-searing throat flashes of red, those shadowy nimbuses cast around them by vibrating wings; be-jeweling the flowering old buckeye, itself a thing of beauty unaided!

Of course, it is of the Ruby-throated Hummingbird I speak. This is the only variety of North American Hummers to be found east of the Mississippi. You can distinguish the males readily from their mates by the gem of ruby the former wear on the throat. Blinding as is that gem's sudden flash, only when the bird faces directly at you can it be seen. Not only do the males return north earlier, after the manner of several other species of birds, but they depart for the south long before mother Hummer can get away, even if she wished. In this latter peculiarity, I believe the Ruby-throat is unique among American birds. I know of no other cases of premature desertion; and this high-handed and casual departure of the male is hard to account for. Neither food scarcity nor frost can be given as reasons. But just try to find one ruby-bearer after September 1st north of the Pennsylvania line! From my own observations and from books, I am able to offer another challenge: try to see a male Hummer feeding his offspring! Evidently he counts his chickens before they're hatched, and afterward he completely loses track. An unregenerate is this dapper fairy, who takes parenthood no more seriously than a bullfrog. As a personal exhibitor of all his traits and oddities, the Ruby-throat has dealt well with me. No bird has quite so thoroughly shown off the intimate habits which one usually has to delve into books to learn of.

To go back to the neighborhood of the old buckeye again: a few weeks after the blooms had withered and the leaves had come out in tufted green, the Hummers who had elected to dwell roundabout began their courtships. Have you seen the manœuvre which distinguishes Hummingbird wooing from all other seduction on earth? As if he were a pendulum-bob, suspended on an invisible wire from a nonexistent point above, the gallant swings back and forth, back and forth, in a fixed arc of perhaps a dozen feet. In front of him, and quite unnoticed at first by the observer, the demure ladylet perches and preens and—we must guess—enjoys this spectacle. An excited chippering on his part continues while he hangs there in the air swaying steadily to and fro. And the hum he makes sounds not unlike bowing on a cello-string. He keeps it up, seeming not to vary his arc at all, oscillating on and on until he sets you fairly dizzy. Such wooing must be effective, else he wouldn't do it year after year! Further convincing proof is that irresistible and lilliputian bit of a nest that turns up shortly—provided you know where to search for it.

I have seen them gathering from boulders and ancient board fences the gray-green lichen bits with which they shingle that nest. I have watched them plucking fern-cotton and cat-tail plush for building its walls. I have been seated on a porch while Mrs. Hummer came several times to carry home a goodly supply of tangled spider-webs, the better to bind on her lichens. Also I have been eyewitness when a white tomcat was driven incontinently from the field by an angry Hummer. I can testify that crows and hawks are sometimes told to move on in no uncertain terms by this pugnacious little champion of home-rights. Yes, they have dealt well with me; I can recommend making their acquaintance!

That actually these garden-haunting birdlets are denizens of the woods appears not generally understood. They are most often seen at the flowerbeds and porch vines. But they come only to feed and be gone. They nearly always make a home among the big trees of a forest or in a quiet old orchard. When you are walking along the edge of a piece of woods or following the bed of a brawling forest brook, and you hear a hard-to-locate squeak; if it is about mid-June, then you might look more closely at the lower horizontal limbs of the white oaks or maples. If either of the Ruby-throats are at home—and they prefer not to be "at home" until the female has begun to brood the pair of unbelievably tiny eggs laid several days before—they will resent your coming near. By their resentment they will show you the lichen-thatched nest they are so nervous about, making its site the center of darting flights in your vicinity. Although few American citizens besides those who are active naturalists have seen a nest, it is not too difficult to locate one after suspicions are fairly well centered upon a definite area. This cup of cottony felt will look not unlike a knot upon its swinging branch, a knot the size of your thumb. After you have found your first, others are sure to come easy, for, as I have said, the birds usually reveal the spot themselves. A little patience and this semi-mythical nest, with its two white beans posing as eggs, will crystallize into reality, and you will have experienced one of the most delightful contretemps in Nature.

After hatching, the feeding of the insect-size babies can be watched without any difficulty or stealth. The mother will come and hover at the nest-side—the father has by now gone the way of his sex and will seldom, if ever, appear—and she will thrust her needle of a bill deep down the nestlings' throats and regurgitate their predigested meal. A process a bit startling to see! As they become larger, the youngsters have tiny spiders added to their menu, as well as undigested nectar. Of course, it is not honey which Hummingbirds get from flowers or, for that matter, bees either—but *nectar*. Honey is a bee-made product.

A common belief is that Hummingbirds rarely alight. But, on the contrary, they spend a relatively small fraction of their time awing, taking frequent rests between flower probings. Because they are so very inconspicuous when resting, they are seldom noticed. A lonely pair of telephone wires spanning a thicket near my home used to be a regular hangout for birds, and there a diminutive Hummer used to bask in the sun half-hours at a stretch.

Three years ago I found a nest on June 20th in a white oak grove. It was, as is usual, near the end of a sloping lower branch—and eleven inches back from it on the same branch was the ruins of a last year's abode! These fragments were grayed and bleached as if surely weatherworn for a whole year, or else I should have supposed them to be merely the foundations of a half-completed nest on a site they had decided to abandon a few weeks previous. But I was forced to believe both nests the work of the same pair. Imagine, if you can, that few cubic centimeters of avian life emigrating in September, immigrating in May; Canada to San Salvador and return; coming straight to the old home over countless miles of journey! Such a midget finding after nine months such a knot-like thing as a Hummingbird's nest!

Please go with me to Southern California for a moment! There I have enjoyed a Hummingbird of a different sort. Anna's Hummingbird is to the West Coast what the Ruby-throat is to the Northeast. But it is more—for the Westerner can *sing!*

Visions of gem-like things rise naturally in your thoughts when you hear the word "Hummingbird." Perhaps you think of those marvelous, glittering winged beings in Bohemian spun-glass—not uncommon once, now alas, extinct. Or possibly you imagine "fragments of a rainbow feast" such as Queen Mab and Oberon may have shared during the height of their empire's glory. When, after becoming thoroughly acquainted with them out-of-doors, the esthetic satisfaction derived from watching them would seem largess enough from *one* store of beauty. But to hear a Hummingbird *sing*—is it not too much? To imagine a sunbeam giving out an odor of attar of rose, or to fancy a flashing drop of dew tasting like honey from Hymettus—thus to an Easterner would it be, did he expect these California jewels to emit a song!

A mite of a creature, plumaged like the delicate abalone shells one finds on Pacific shores, competing with bulbul, nightingale and skylark! Yes, an American Hummer is one of the world's fine songsters—albeit in its own sweet way. There is not in Nature's repertoire a jollier, more rollicking madrigal than is troubadored by Anna's Hummingbird. What an inadequate name! Who Anna was, whether queen or naturalist or wife, rocking the cradle or the ship of state, history revealeth not.

In the cloudless California winter he perches

with cocky diminutiveness on palm frond, cedar-tip or eucalyptus twig. A hundred times an hour his needle-like elfin carol rings out:

> Deedle dee dee
> Deedle dee dee—
> Oh, gee! Oh, gee! Oh, gee!

It is exactly the sort of sound you once expected to hear from brownies or fairies, when happily you should chance to surprise a group dancing in the moonlight. No insect voice is keener and farther-going; though its timbre resembles cricket, grasshopper or locust not at all. It carries through the greenery about you like the shrillest of tiny whistles. Neither its tone nor its richness make it irresistible; it is the rollicking gaiety of it which captivates you. Quite as his song pierces the foliage, so does the sudden flash of his violet throat hit your eye-balls. You are at first incredulous that you interpreted the color aright. Could it really have been such a violet flame! Ah, there it is again, more flaming than before! Such color, such expression of delight, such whole-hearted caroling! The ditty is poured out, almost forced out, one could say, from his ecstatic body. Every fibre is aquiver with the effort. This avian Tom Thumb is all atwitter with some excitement within, some injunction which is laid upon him to tell the whole world how extraordinary life is.

Watch as he alights upon the tiptop of a twenty-foot cedar. Ah, there is another—his mate! a demure replica of him! on a demure perch well below his! Now we begin to understand the affair! Sitting there, he squeaks once his "Deedle dee dee" but does not finish the ditty. Up, straight up, he goes. Up, until the blue depths all but lose him. All of a sudden, with folded wings, he falls like a stone from heaven. When almost down to her level, and with a quick brake of wings, he stops at the end of a short swoop. From the taughtened feathers comes a *zinging*, brazen whir-r-r. Like a dart which the eye cannot follow, he has settled himself upon the same cedar-tip from which he launched, bursting into a fairly breathless "Oh, gee! Oh, gee! Oh, gee!" . . . Then a microscopic flirt of wings, a diminutive preen of fairy-like plumage. Look, he is off again! The daredevil slide is repeated, only to end in his settling, light as thistledown, upon the twig he left.

Eight, nine, ten times the caper is repeated—until he is either convinced of a duty well performed or too tired to go on. The gossamer feathers are preened again with exceeding care and at great length. He will sit and view the world for a time. But he simply cannot contain himself. In spite of obvious effort to check it, out will come every few minutes a burst of rapture that will not down.

Years afterward, when by chance you hear a squeak of crystal glassware rubbed tightly together, you will surely recall with a start a far California glade steeped in sunshine, and a freeholder of fairyland piping his gay Jubilate.

East or West, the smallest of the birds has yielded me the largest number of pages in my notebooks. And thus far, I have never seen in the open but two kinds of Hummingbirds out of the scores between Manitoba and Patagonia!

Owls and Owls

THE plump old darky suddenly fell upon her knees in the dooryard. Repeatedly bowing her head to the ground, she began to wail in heart-rending distress. Astonished, I hastened up the path toward her.

This was several autumns ago in the back-country of the Catskills. Toiling up a steep hill-road, I had seen ahead of me this typical Old Mammy trudging along, basket on arm, shawl over shoulders. I had nearly caught up to her when she turned down a lane toward a ramshackle cabin back from the road. No sooner had she waddled to within speaking distance of it, than she amazed me by falling on her knees. Like King David of old, her hands made the motions of casting ashes upon her sinful head.

"Oh, Lawd!" she moaned, "Oh, Lawd! Doan take him from me yit, doan take him from me yit!" Now and again her outbursts redoubled in anguish when she would steal a glance at the cabin. I could get no clue to the mystery. I came to her side with an offer of help; but my unheard approach startled her half out of her senses. "OH!"

she shrieked. Then, "Oh, is dat *you?*—de man acomin' up de road jes' now? . . . Trouble? Trouble? . . . Man, doan yo' see hit up dar! . . . My ole man gotter go, he shuah gotter go!"

I looked again—then I saw "hit." The little brick chimney, arched over so that a triangular opening had been left on two sides, sheltered a small gray ball. From either side of the ball rose a thin stream of smoke—truly, it was an uncanny effect! This was Mammy's Nemesis—a dozing Screech Owl. He sat there as unconcerned at his satanic surroundings as if he were dreaming of squirrel meat, himself deep in the privacy of a hollow tree-trunk. With horn-like ear-tufts and closed eyes with dark orbits, he presented a symbol of Judgment striking to behold.

I touched her gently on the shaking shoulder. "Mother, it's a gray one up there. Look again. Only red ones fetch bad luck—this one's gray."

Taking one more furtive look at the chimney, her fear vanished. "Bress yo', suh, bress yo'. I done fohgit dat. Yo's right, shu'!" And she arose and went on her way rejoicing.

I felt that I had looked upon a myth in the making. I might have been transported for a moment to some Caribbean island. Here was a harking back straight to primordial voodoo. Through some such wild fable as this Xantyltl was chosen, perhaps; and Pawpawkeewis, Ganesh, Hathor. In this fashion must have originated most of the animistic fables and witchcraft tabus of the world. First the fear, then the fable, then the worship of the fable. "Man lives not by bread alone, but mainly by catchwords," philosophized R. L. S. Yes, even today, man lives not alone by fact, but mostly by fetich: by the "holy words" cast around the styles, food fads, cosmetics, militarism, advertising, the divine right of wealth—and what not—all with as little foundation in thinking as had this idea of Mammy's.

Likewise, the step is short betwixt Poetry and Falsehood. To call a downy ten-inch owl an omen infernal might be a striking figure of speech in *Paradise Lost;* to a naturalist it is mere superstition. So gentle a gray elf to be linked with mankind's devils, his fears and ignorance! Mammy's sky-blue imagination simply rushed in where objective common sense, being absent, had left a vacuum. As sensible for her to discriminate in favor of gray-phased as against red-phased owls, as it was to connect owls at all with her voodoo creed. Why a red-feathered bird is the more portentous is hard to see; yet such seems to be a fixed belief among many of the best Aframerican families. Not only in black minds but in white. Don't we all prefer our devils red? Mammy's white co-religionists are legion. Medieval Christianity may have developed its concept of a horned devil from the owl model, rather than from horned bull or tusked boar, animals of daylight, too familiar to be supernatural. A thorough thirteenth-century astrologer could scarcely have thought of setting up shop without an owl, caged or stuffed. As for Halloween, that pagan hangover from pre-Christian Europe, what would modern shop-keepers do in October without the witch and the owl!

But there are causes if not reasons for the owl's place in wizardry. Creatures of the night. Incarnations of solemnity. Away back in the Golden Age of Athens, owls were minted upon coins as symbols of the wisdom and omniscience of the state, and as an honor to Minerva. And down through the years, they have symbolized luck, magic, mystery, secrecy, calamity, and prophecy. At Macbeth's death, "It was the owl that shriek'd, the fatal bellman which gives the stern'st goodnight."

Evolution decreed that owls should be nocturnal. This alone is enough to have nominated them as witches' assistants. Those who are out much o' nights readily acquire a reputation for being deep ones. Also, those who "don't say much" but look knowing, accumulate great respect for shrewdness. Moreover, those who hear all that goes on around them cannot escape learning a thing or two. The old owl that sat in the oak, "The less he spoke, the more he heard," has solid basis in fact. . . . How suited their voices; their cat's eyes of brightest yellow; their wings shod with silence; are to the night and the darkness thereof! The Psalmist might have sung of them that "their ways are ways of silentness, and all their paths are peace"—if by peace is meant stillness. One Barn Owl that I pulled from a giant knothole and brought home to observe at leisure, used to fly distractedly back and forth through the low attic, eighteen-inch wings all but striking my head. I could feel the fanning of the air, but could not hear the sound of its wing-strokes. It was a ghostly performance. This silent hunting enables them to strike unsuspecting prey like a dart from a Pygmy's blowpipe. They are minions of the Silent Death. The buzzing wing-beat of crows passing over or the whirring flight sounds of ducks, herons and hawks, are audible a good distance away. Not so an owl's. The latter loses a certain swiftness of flight as the price of this stillness, because the fine filaments of down covering edges and tips of his pinions lessen the wings' driving power. The resulting slightly labored motion will give a practiced eye sufficient clue as to a distant bird so that an owl can be distinguished invariably from crow or hawk.

We discover in America two types of owls: the round-headed and the ear-tufted. The sense of hearing might be expected to be more keen in the ear-tufted varieties: Screech Owl, Long-eared Owl and Great-Horned Owl—but it has never been demonstrated. Round-heads, like the Acadian, Barred, Barn, and the winter visitor, the Great Gray Owl, seem to have equally good microphones. The hearing of the whole tribe is astonishingly acute. A hound's nose can track you across a sand dune twenty-four hours later. A turkey buzzard's eye will detect the carcass of a woodchuck from a mile above. Ten minutes after it has been tossed out, a dozen will be standing-by, though not a buzzard may have been noticed for days. A Barn Owl will hear and pursue a mouse scampering across the dry leaves of a forest-floor several hundred yards away. These miracles I have seen. But first prize goes to a Screech Owl which one winter twilight I was watching through a pair of binoculars. He was perched perhaps sixty feet from the ground in a leafless birch. Suddenly, near me in some thick cedar scrub, a roosting Junco fluttered the tiniest feather as it settled itself for the night. In a flash, coming almost straight toward where I lay, making a perfectly curved parabola, the little hunter shot into the tangle and flew off with the bird in its talons. It was an act not aided by sight; it was all hearing. The distance covered in that swoop was at least eighty yards. At another time—in early evening, too—while walking home on an Adirondack trail through hemlock saplings crowding the pathway, my fur cap was mysteriously jerked from my head like lightning and dropped a few feet away. I just caught a glimpse of a swift and hungry Great-Horned Owl as it shot away through the trees. My padding feet had made no sound, and he, perched above, and hearing the rustling branch-lets, had simply pounced on what he must have mistaken for a furry animal among the hemlocks.

And as for voices! Some day, it may be, a painter will portray the four Great Sadnesses symbolized by that shy quartette of our eastern woods: the Great Horned, the Barred, the Barn, and the Screech Owl. For the first he will depict the form of a wild, boisterous, rollicking she-devil, one to whose mad despondency blue frost is as flame and blizzards as breezes from the sun. For the second, he will show a rustic maid, throat-choked with love's despair, giving way to utter grief amid the forest solitudes. The third would be a country wife, work-enslaved into dumb hopelessness to which she must give voice what time the green comes again to upland pastures. For the last, there could be only some young mother's sorrow wailed above the grave of her firstborn son. Unearthly voices, lugubrious voices! When they do express vocally their "deep, deep, deep thoughts"—the sound seems to come from the sticky depths of corrupt decay. Thoreau thought it "expressive of a mind which has reached the gelatinous, mildewy stage in the mortification of all healthy and courageous thought." Obvious anthropomorphism; but perfect description. . . . A sardonic laughter, a scream of anguish, a hoot of derision, a hysterical baying at the moon: these form the bulk of the vocabulary of a seemingly degenerate branch of birddom—only that "degenerate" is palpable anthropomorphism too.

Appropriately, in keeping with such voices, owls habitually regurgitate much of what they swallow; ejecting in pellets the fur, bones and teeth of prey which they have hurriedly bolted whole. A ghoulish practice; one which may have figured heavily in our ancient indictment of owls as devil's assistants! A hunting owl will gulp his mouse, squirrel or insect; and, after digestion, will disgorge neat, hard, oval pellets, compressed with a laboratory niceness. Actually they catch more than they eat when they get the chance. Their eyes are larger than their stomachs. I have several times seen a Barn Owl sitting patiently in some dim nook amid the rafters, with half the tail of a rat projecting from its beak, the more nutritious portion of the rodent undergoing the processes of alimentation further down. They have all day for digestion. An owl works while we sleep; then his stomach works while he sleeps. . . . Were one to search for nests, there is no surer indication of the inhabitancy of a suspected eyrie than these pellets scattered beneath and near by. Likewise, each of their lookout places—or, rather, listening-posts—in the woods has dotted below it remnants of their ravenous feasts; resident owls having regular nightly beats for hunting. If the hapless creatures which form their prey noted the pellets and torn remnants and took due warning, it would be well for them. But they never do: an owl hoots, they start with fear—and it is all up with them! Owl cries seem intended to produce sudden consternation, a jump and a scurry for cover, which movements be they ever so slight, the owl's wonderfully acute ears detect.

I do not believe that the human sort of fear exists among animals; a fear characterized by apprehension and dread. The animal fear is only a brief reaction, a quick panic in face of overt danger. Animals have no conception of death, and do not sense it in imagination as a mortal in peril would do. I have never seen what I could call a *scared* owl: and no evidence indicating that he who would instill terror by his voice knows that emotion himself. In fact, all predatory animals show concern in the face of danger only by a heightened vigilance and a trembling readiness for escape. It is asserted by experimenters in zoological gardens that rabbits, guinea pigs and mice put into reptile cages as food show no fear of quiet or dormant snakes, but will frisk and play about their coils unmindful of the fate in store for them.

One winter I was well entertained by an instance of daring on the part of a red-phase Screecher whom I removed day after day from a roosting cavity. While I was carrying him home, he played 'possum in the usual manner. Then I would let him suddenly start up from my hand and fly back to the woods. At last, becoming tired of such petty tyranny, I was on the point of stopping the game, when one morning, after three days of heavy snowfall, I called for him, but he was missing. At noon a farmer down the road brought me an owl he had struck down with a horse-whip in his barn just after the culprit had killed one of his prize Rhode Island cocks. He brought the latter along, too, and we found the actual weight of the owl to be one-sixth that of the rooster. Never thereafter finding Screecher in his stump, I concluded it was doubtless he whom hunger had driven to such a reckless act. He had died with his claws on, as it were.

The difference of coloration (i.e., phase) in animals of the same species is baffling to account for —just as freckles and red hair are. Every farm boy discovers that some woodchucks are quite black, although most are brownish gray; and he knows his sooty lamb to be an accident: a black sheep in the family. For several generations, even scientists thought the "Black Squirrel" a distinct species; not merely a brunette Gray Squirrel. Skunks vary widely in the amount of white markings; individuals being trapped all the way from nearly pure white to solid black. The Adirondack Black Bear has a similar penchant for going tan. This difference in phase is apparently unrelated to the phenomenon known as "Albinism"; or to the change from winter to summer coats. An Albino, of course, has from birth no normal pigment in his system; so its skin and eyes are pink owing to the blood's shining through and its hair is white. Certain birds and animals in northern United States (such as the Ptarmigans and Snowshoe Rabbits) replace a summer garb with an entirely different winter one, and so achieve protective coloration. But the phase problem concerns itself with creatures of the same species and sex varying in color *from one another*.

Among birds the most striking example is that of our common Screech Owl. The study of his case has led only to as intelligent a conclusion as the black Catskill Mammy put her faith in: investigators avering that either a *true species* is *disintegrating* into two right before our eyes; or that two distinct species are *amalgamating* directly under our noses. You might, offhand, conclude that it would be easy to decide through experiment—but it isn't, for the pure-bloodedness of your breeding-stock is always in question, in the first place. And there are further obstacles. Such, for example, as whether the food of captive birds has anything to do with the matter. Or lack of proper exercise. . . .

The Screech Owl plumage "comes" in two different shades, though each presents the same pattern. Some are red, some are gray; quite as some of us are light-haired or dark. Both shades are equally good protection. The red phase appears from reports to occur oftener south of central New York than north of it. . . . "Warm skies, warm skin?" Or was there, perhaps, a "Norman invasion" of Owl-land, in which blond hordes from the north swept in and, by subjugating and later fraternizing with the natives, as the Normans did, engendered a new race? Is the little gray owl destined to supplant his dark-hued rival?—even as the light-haired and blue-eyed Teutonic "freak" of the pre-Roman era has now spread south and west, and is one day to dominate the complexions of the world? Or, contrariwise, is it as arguable that the swarthy devotees of some raptorial Mohammed have yet to meet their Charles Martel and be turned back? There is no telling at present.

Eugenists contend that never a baby had darker hair than its darkest haired parent, and that dark eyes never yet sprung from a parental union of "true" (i.e. pure) blonds. Such Mendelian law may also hold true for Screech Owls—at least, I have yet to see a nestful of young of mixed coloration unless the parent birds differed in phase. Nevertheless, cases have been vouched for on reputable authority.

Here is a field for careful exploration. One ornithologist thinks a diet of crayfish has something to do with it: yet surely if one of a pair ate crayfish, the other one would, too. To make the whole thing more baffling, it is stated by certain authorities that captives have been known to *change* phase in the aviary! May not a leopard change its spots? Is such a change in a caged owl due to age, food, sorrow, sunlight, or—what?

Fall and winter is the best time to start cultivating the Screech Owl's acquaintance. This tiny preyer, rarely seen or heard from March to August, miraculously multiplies himself so that by the evening of the first white frost, it is a forsaken countryside, indeed, where the wails of several cannot be heard condoling with one another's sorrows. (However, during 1930 I heard a neighborhood pair every week from June to—well, up until New Year's.) In October the parents, with the six or seven grown offspring, discovering just about this time the use of their voices, are doubtless a terror to migrating small birds. In the early autumn the family often commence hunting before it is fully dark, picking up many a luckless migrant as it flies in to perch for the night. I have several times seen and heard the silent watchers catch a dozing bird in the deepening twilight—they themselves readily concealed in the adjacent foliage. In daylight the clamor of robins, jays, warblers and other small fry, who have suddenly discovered the grim sleeper among the leaves, will lead you to find him.

When the foliage drops, then tactics change. It then becomes largely a question of mice and the stalking of hedgerows and fence tangles. Also, now the owl must seek a cavity to hide in during the day, for he can no longer skulk in shady nooks. If one's enthusiasm be unquenchable enough to force him to climb to and peer down all likely-looking tree cavities in the locality, a winter is sure to yield a Screech Owl or two. In early morning they may often be spied with head and shoulders filling the entrance like an odd sort of knot on the tree. Usually they play dead when hauled out of a hole, often letting a comical little whine escape their clenched beak. But give them a chance, and, like a greased pig, they slip from your hands, and wild-eyed, with ear-tufts erect and bill snapping, betake themselves to cover. They never offer to bite with that hooked bill, but are pathetically nonresistant. Often the surplus prey of the night before is taken into the roosting cavity, and you will find your owl has been standing on a mouse or bird all day long.

Another nonconformity of the owl clan is the

trait most species have of laying their round white eggs so early in the year. The Great Horned Owl, who ranges the whole continent, lays its eggs the earliest of all birds. In the extreme south it even mixes up the calendar to the extent of beginning its set in mid-December. What keeping warm these two or three billiard-balls means when the thermometer in this part of the world works in negative numbers, is not given us weakling mortals to know. Many of this owl's youngsters are hatched with ice chunks for play-things and with March winds to caress them. In northern New York I have found these fuzzy owlets lying on ice-lined nests—once in the second week of March! Somewhat in the manner that Anarctic explorers describe the King Penguin as holding its single egg off the ice by enfolding it between its thick webbed feet and body, must the Great Horned Owl protect its two or three from freezing. Only, the owls must make their fluffy leg-feathering take the part of webbed feet. To leave the nest for a few minutes when the temperature is at zero means that the eggs crack. Although Screechers are not so impatient with the seasons as that, their nesting is early: it begins in New England about April first. The babies emerge four weeks later. Such big and aggressive birds as the *raptores* need a long growing-season. A very prudent silence is maintained around Screecher's home: a hole just large enough for them to squeeze into, and discreetly out of the way of cats and noise. To see a group of the fuzzy gray gnomes sitting statuesquely close together along a bare limb—before most migrant birds have even returned north—is a grotesque spectacle.

There is something challenging in the all-year-roundness of owls. There is outstanding perseverance, self-sufficiency, determination. Especially thrilling is it to encounter them in winter when food-winning is the real thing, and most birds have given up the battle and gone away south. Every afternoon during November and December a few years ago, I had to walk home in the gloaming below the east side of a wooded ridge. Sharply silhouetted against the delicately tinted sky, the trees above were etched in black. Almost daily as I passed, a Long-eared Owl used to quit his hiding place and wing swiftly along over the tree-tops, a dark, flickering shadow. In the lonely, frosty dusk, he carried a depressing foreboding of cold, hunger and suffering yet to come. Yet, he "carried on" and brought himself through the bitterest February I have ever experienced.

Although they are of the breed of the Boones and Carsons—woodsmen and pioneers who cannot stand being elbowed by neighbors and retreat everywhere before the intrusion of the white man's settlements—the larger owls once in a while do linger in strange places. Perhaps it is only because they are attached through years of association to a certain piece of timber—like the pair that a few years back nested in a bit of thick woods near my former home. These woods are actually but twenty miles from Columbus Circle, Manhattan. When I first settled in this locality, I used to hear them hoot in winter nights; a throaty "Whooo, whooo, whooo, whoo-ah!" that might readily have passed for a dog's barking. The following May, in these woods above which the shifting searchlight from a Fifth Avenue skyscraper swings its finger of ghostly light, I had the thrill of watching an entire family of four, the twins nearly three-fourths grown, vainly trying to hide themselves among the leafing treetops. They have a curiously *overgrown* style of head, due to the large black sockets encircling the eyes, and their mein was one of comical gravity. They peered down with an expression of mingled anxiety and disapproval ludicrous in the extreme. But, alas, after five years of real-estate developments and county boulevards, the woods sheltered them no more.

My personal acquaintance with the Acadian, or

"Saw-whet" Owl was a long-deferred privilege.
Once twenty years ago, beside Lake Ontario, I had
heard that rasping shriek, filing away at the saw
that ever seems to need sharpening, but did not
see the bird at that midnight hour. The noise was
unmistakeable; saw-whetting describes it well
enough. But if you do not happen to be something
of a carpenter, you might not know what filing a
saw sounds like. A long, thin "wheeeep" of a
sound, turned up a little at both ends,—that's as
near as I can put it. The actual meeting with the
bird, however, took place only three years ago.
That was in western Pennsylvania on March 19th.
The encounter was a notable one. For, in the first
place, this is the second smallest owl in America;
the smallest east of the Mississippi. Then, again,
if the species be not lawfully classed as very rare,
it is indeed seldom one is seen. Their daylight habits are so retiring, their size so easily overlooked,
that few ornithologists see them. Though I have
covered a good bit of ground myself in the past
three decades, I have seen a Saw-whet but twice
and heard one but four times.

It was a warm morning. I was sitting on the
thick dry leafage of a small thicket, watching two
Mourning Cloak butterflies just emerged and cele-
brating resurrection among the first Hepaticas. My

interest was caught after a while by a near-by Tufted Titmouse who seemed oddly and untit-mousely fidgety at every sound or movement I made. Something was not just right in the neigh-borhood, and he felt it. A sharp alarm-note from a Chickadee made him bolt precipitously into a grapevine tangle. No sooner had he done so than he bolted out again and began chattering in high excitement. A brace of Chickadees aided him, and in no time at least fifteen nearby birds came tilting to the spot.

There must be a Screech Owl in that grape tangle, I thought, and proceeded to investigate. What I saw just over my head, gave me also a start. What a small Screech Owl! And what an off-shade of rufous!—No ear-tufts, either! Why—it's a Saw-whet Owl! (Instant identification was possible because it is the only little owl in eastern United States which does not sport the expressive ear-tuft.) He regarded me—not haughtily, with-eringly, as a Screecher would—but in a comically petulant manner, cocking his head doubtfully at every change in my position. He was scarcely able to make me out at all in the bright sunshine; al-though his eyes grew their roundest in the effort. When a Screech Owl looks coldly at you, you feel that he sees you well enough, the brilliant yellow of his irises heightening the keen-eyed effect. But this raptorial pygmy lacked that intense yellow iris, his were almost a brown. The *round,* full pupils and the odd pencilings radiating around the eye-sockets, like "crows' feet," gave them a hollow-eyed look.

About three-quarters the size of his second-cousin, Screech Owl, this worried little brownie up there probably did not weigh as much as a robin, yet a certain dignity sat upon him. He was a killer, an eater of meat and drinker of blood, a pouncer, a pursuer; these things showed in his mien and carriage. This dignity, together with the round "owl-shaped" head, gave the effect of adding ounces and inches to his frame. Five or six broad stripes of rich dull brown on a background of white, varied his chest markings from Screecher's, whose frontage is mottled.

I recalled a pair of Florida Screech Owls I succeeded in catching in a little deserted barn near Jacksonville. One was gray, the other red, and they were both smaller than the northern variety. Saw-whet, here, was exactly their size—but a Round-head instead of a Cavalier. Their eye-balls were vertical slits, his circular; their tufts, like mustachios, stood straight up; his poll was rounded like a friar's.

As I walked around and around the tangle, he screwed his head in circles, too,—or seemed to, in that remarkable way an owl has. Only, of course, popular and ignorant legend to the contrary, he accomplished the sleight-of-neck by zipping the head back from the half-way position so quickly that often my eye could not catch the whirl. Otherwise, I could have "wrung his neck"—as I have been assured you can by walking repeatedly around him. He permitted me to set him swaying gently up and down by pulling at a branch; but did not offer flight. I was as much a curiosity to him as he was to me. Finally, when I nearly put my hand upon him, he flew, silent as a moth, to a second vine tangle twenty yards off, thereby subjecting himself to a most insulting review by a corps of indignant Chickadees and Tits.

I took occasion to explore the terrain of the vicinity, noting promising holes and cavities where later I might call to meet the other half of the elfin pair. But though I did come back several times later I did not locate the nest site, and so my first Acadian passed out of my life forever—that is, unless you call these pages a ghost of him!

He Would A-hawking Go

THE Fowler was going a-hawking.

Alas, not with red-haired Queen Bess, nor yet with Sir Walter Raleigh, and, in sooth, never with any of the roistering baronets of this county Suburbia (whose falconing is done better than his by their golden double-eagles!)—nay, he must needs go unhorsed and alone. For, save these ghosts from history, there were none he might bid be comrade!

Not yet is it a lost art, this coursing; although the wise encyclopedias of 1930 say that Hawking, beloved of knight and rajah, is a sport which languished with the Stuarts. The dainty task of "fitting your hawks their jesses" is to be done, the books tell us, forevermore only in poetry. But authority is not seldom mistaken. Hawking has survived—at least, in one eager breast—just as this one Patron Fowler has pursued it these many springs.

He caught himself singing softly while he dressed, with obligato shivers operating up and down his spine, in the five o'clock gloom of the

April morning. When he noticed his humming, the song was just ending about certain high roads and low roads to Loch Lomond; and he realized that an inner jubilation had laid hold upon him. For if a man sing unawares, surely a keen anticipation is lying in wait just around the corner. Be the business depression what it would, there was no cloud over this April dawn. Today the Fowler had a more flourishing enterprise afoot.

For he was going a-hawking. Silken palfries, gay satins, flaring gauntlets, servile retinue, alone, never did make Hawking a sport of kings, and their absence now detracted not a whit from it. Today's Hawking has but few and simple requirements. One essential—not too common these clockwork days—recommends it over all other avocations, even business-building and golf: hawking waxes only in the rising sun, golf and dividends await the going of the dew. Only milking-time on the farm begins as early; they who hawk must start betimes, for their hunting is long.

The night just passed had been fairly pulsing with the distant chorus of the hylas in the marsh outside, soothing the ears like a lullaby—"a ghost of sleighbells in a mist of snow." It had been a heavy, foggy, mysterious night such as only mid-April can lay over a troubled world. All outdoors

had been feverishly working, working, at the ten
thousand various labors that must be accomplished
ere spring be thoroughly established in the land.
Nature was extending herself to make up for time
lost by a fortnight of frosts.

Sap was pushing to its twig-limits in every tree;
buds were swelling rapidly; frogs were unearth-
ing and starting forth for the nearest swamp;
feminine Robins and Bluebirds had been passing
north all night to join lustier mates gone on two
weeks before; flock after flock of Juncoes, White-
throats and Blackbirds had also winged the upper
damp air since darkness fell. Muskrats had begun
digging holes in the creek bank, against an inevitable rise of freshet waters soon to render their
winter quarters deathtraps. Bloodroot and Liverwort were growing in the warm dark, as avidly as
antler-velvet grows on deer-buck, to be ready for
the blossoming rite almost at hand. A Screech Owl
over in the next orchard was sitting out the last
few days of maternal vigil. Through the darkness
a Loon had gone by, laughing *sotto voce*, in sub-
dued glee at its home-coming. Ducks and herons
had slipped by in swift companies at the directions
of captains giving stealthy orders. . . . It had
been a night full of cheeps, squawks, quacks, rust-
les and splashes—sounds hard to classify or dis-

tinguish one from the other. And, in consequence, the Fowler had slept but fitfully. . . . Yet, in spite of this, here he was humming happily at five A.M.

Hawking, Old Style, required that you take with you your hawk to hunt; Hawking, New Style, demands that you go out and hunt your hawk—and everything else is game that falls to the hunting. Hawking, Old Style, was the diversion of kings and landed lords; Hawking, new style, is sport which any American sovereign may follow if he will. Old Style Hawking was set for autumn; in the new style, you sally forth only in spring. In the Old Style days, Hawkers went forth in troops and merry companies; the new styler travels alone, or—God being good—with one who understands. In Hawking, Old Style, your falcon climbed to the skies in pursuit of his prey; in New Style Hawking you climb, praying at times, skyward after your falcon. Once your hand was leather-shod to carry the hawk; nowadays your feet must be shod with steel spurs that carry you to the hawk.

Properly accoutered, the Fowler started off down the road. The waking cocks were challenging one another to produce a finer comb and a neater tail. What a roomy jubilance in such crow-ing! It seems to carry, rich and resonant, ten times as far as in summer and fall. What an adaptive immigrant, this one hundred per cent American, late from tropic jungle, to be calling boldly over sponge-wet and snow-patched landscape! Is his spring voice really stronger and lustier, we wonder, or does vernal air amplify the sound and the past weeks of white quietness heighten it?

Barely had the first quarter-mile been left behind when that free-swinging, devil-may-care voice came from the clouds: the cry which Hawkers can never hear unmoved. What contrast between a rooster's crow and a Red-shouldered Hawk's spring call! One the acme of domesticity, the other of wildness. A subtle chord there is in the latter, vibrating with mountains, forests, lakes and clean freedom, which sets ringing within us a sympathetic overtone of longing. The hawk seems to have retained a primordial soul and spirit of fire, the which, as a common inheritance, humanity has long since lost. Here and there some incorrigible mortal trails clouds of its glory; some lovable anarchist who moves as in a nimbus of recalled liberty, answerable only to his raptorial—not *rapacious*—instincts. Mankind has developed a pampered body, an intellect, a society, a printing press, an all-but Frankenstein government; but the evolution of the hawk has winged along more unhampered lines. He has kept mainly to the heights; to the serenities above earthly moil. We who have traded such a birthright as his for a pottage of civilization envy him who hath given away all that he had—and remained a hawk!

High up in the clear blue morning they swung, the pair of them, making the air resound with hearty life. Again they had returned, the Fowler's acquaintances of many a spring. Peculiar tricks of voice, or odd and unusual markings on eggs examined in the same nest year after year, present convincing evidence that for decades the self-same pair of hawks do come back to the same woodlands. Not always—for there is the accuracy of modern shotguns and the inaccuracy of the mental mechanisms which aim at them!

Red-shouldered Hawks, one of eight raptorial varieties common in the eastern states, serve as epitomes of all hawkdom. Thoreau spoke of the ubiquitous fresh-water Perch as typifying "the fish principle in nature." Perch were, he asserted, the composite, ideal, all-round *fish*, occupying the average or general environment; the expression of what a living organism must necessarily become where water, sun, algæ and tiny prey are set as a stage for its appearance. . . . The Red-shoul-

der exemplifies the hawk principle in nature. Just
as the Crow is the best adapted, least specialized,
most composite *bird*, which can live anywhere and
feed upon anything, so this hawk is the summa-
tion of the raptore family; the highest common
divisor, as it were, of all the species all over the
earth. In his wings lies the soaring power of the
race, his beak and talons are characteristic of all
raptores, his voice and manner, the glorification
of all that preying, soaring, wilderness-haunting,
have brought to a bird. His spirit is the spirit
which must evolve when Nature puts such twos
and twos together.

This hawk and his close kin are distributed well
over the globe, and neither the locality they inhabit nor the names they bear affect their mani-
festation of the hawk principle. Whether you
watch him circle and circle over the vine-clad
slopes of the Rhine; or mark his lonely wheeling
across the Arizona sagebrush wastes; or see a pair
weave lofty spirals of silence far above the water-
falls of Switzerland; or look down upon his tilting
back from the green Peak at Hong Kong; or note
him aloft over the eternal Sphinx in the deep-
water blue of Egyptian sky; it is the hawk principle that stirs you, not the feathered bird. He is
a remorseless reminder of a certain regretted great-

ness in man; an incarnation wherein we cringed
before no Pilate and bent no knee before Crœsus.

Thus the Fowler, looking up, wondered what
ultra-mondaine affairs he might not be giving ear
to yonder, high in the great silences:

> Sail ho!—What ship? . . . But on he sails
> By way of the Turquoise Straits,
> For the Archipelago of Clouds
> Steers his celestial freights.
>
> To winds unfelt below
> He trims full sails, and lays
> Straight course ahead to ports unknown;
> Uncharted routes his ways.
>
> . . . What cargo bear ye, bark?
> What wrecks spoke ye at sea?
> Hailed ye my Ships, my golden Ships?—
> What tidings sent they me?

Now, just *why* the Fowler had started out this
April 17th; just *why* he would seek mere hawk's
nests—neglecting the mare's nests of workaday
routine—climb to them, be they never so high, to
glut eyes upon the umber, chestnut and cream-
colored eggs they cradle—perhaps to add them to
his hoard in a big oak cabinet—he cannot explain.
For that matter, did a certain famed Mr. Morgan
ever try to explain, or excuse, his passion for col-

lecting mediæval madonnas and rare government
bonds? Did a certain Buona Tombo Roosevelt attempt to tell exactly why big-game hunting was a
scientific pursuit? Explanation lies somewhere in
the blood and not in the tongue. . . . Let April
come again, and through working and sleeping
hours there begin to pass visions of seventy-five-
foot birches, Gargantuan sugar maples and colos-
sal beeches, in whose tops, unseen normally save
by bird and squirrel, are scaffolded that most alluring of the wood's treasures, a hawk's nest. As
a blind man readily threads the windings of sel-
dom-trod paths and locates landmarks on the
by-ways of former days; so something enables
Fowlers to preserve for years, within a sort of
subconscious limbo, the sites of scores of these
hawk homes. He has but to start down one of the
paths of the compass, and lo, his way becomes a
succession of yesterdays, a highroad whereupon
both sides are the things he has remembered. He
plots a course from tree to tree; a galleon tacking
among the Indies that pay it tribute. . . . During ten months of the year this lore lies dormant
and fallow. Then, something in the April air—
perhaps the same magic that awakes frog and toad
and skunk cabbage far underground—whispers an

Open Sesame, and no fox of the hills is a keener sylvan geographer.

Hawks commonly come to love the structures which the labor of their beaks has builded; they return annually with remarkable tenacity of purpose. And even where they have appropriated an already second-hand eyrie, they often use that repeatedly. At this time of year, what may not turn up in a day's walk? One may look for a dozen varieties of nests: Red-shoulder, Red-tail, Broad-winged, Sharp-shinned, and Cooper's Hawks, the Goshawk, and at least five owls will be at home if he calls. The sprightly little Sparrow Hawk will be getting his house in order for May.

As planned for this day, the round would touch at a dozen regular ports-of-call. Tramp and climb, climb and tramp; from six to six—if the thirst be slaked that burns within. For Hawking is from sun to sun and a Hawker's trips are never done. First, to revisit the flakey-barked old birch standing sentinel over the ravine entrance to Nolan's woods. As long as memory could recall, a pair of Red-tail Hawks had used that nest, each spring adding a few sticks to repair the flattening winter snows had given it, until by now its bulk exceeded by a bushel the orthodox architecture of the species. Three sets of eggs had been collected from this ancient tree, although visits of late years were innocent of acquisitive motive. Yet, perennially the Fowler longed to discover upon unimpeachable authority whether there were to be four eggs or five, and whether this season's laying would show that odd twisting smudge of burnt umber about the larger ends, a mark which had established to a certainty, April after April, a common parentage for the eggs.

Two miles of spring fields and spring dawn; then the ravine's edge, and a sight up along two-and-a-half-score feet of birch trunk. Those long flakes of loosening bark had proved deceptive before. A six-foot scrambling slide at altitude forty, a few years ago, when the climbing spurs failed to strike through to solid cambium wood, nearly deprived the anxious world of an inconsequential naturalist. As it then chanced, a sudden recovery on the tip of one spur enabled him to descend with wrists deeply scratched, a shaken and an humble man. . . . Seizing a fallen branch, the Fowler struck the tree two lusty whacks. A response aloft! But not the response anticipated, for the occupant that whipped from the nest had not the rusty underbody of the expected host. It was a smaller and trimmer raptore—a Cooper's Hawk. So the old tenants had not renewed their lease—ah, shotguns and ignorance! But such a site was too desirable to lie idle in these days of dwindling big trees and expanding thickets. As the interloper flew away, she uttered that cackling scolding which has a unique whirling and swirling quality, as if the sound were being emitted by an object going at tremendous speed. No other hawk has a note like it.

Climbers from rucksack, and up he went, driving yet another series of scars into the long-suffering birch which had so many now. Four dirty-white eggs was the modest contribution to "oological" lore yielded by that struggle. Four to be added to that old oak cabinet; the taker being prompted by motives akin to those which hung up the stags' heads, fox tails and herons' wings hung in many a Tudor-panelled hunting hall. Trophies of the chase men must have, be they shark's teeth, elephant tusks, Teuton helmets, or autographs.

Next, the Fowler tapped incredulously upon a gnarled maple bole, scarred with an encounter of three years previous. There was "nothing stirring." But as his gaze scaled the unrelenting pylon of timber and, musing in wonder at the number of times the tree had changed its mind while growing, he caught sight of a mote in the blue, some-

thing far up between two cottony clouds. A suspicion . . . a hint . . . a certainty! Mother
Red-tail watches over her own, almost invisibly,
lest a greater evil befall *her*. Perhaps some ruthless gun once belched malevolent death at her
from below; slithering, whining death, that ripped
twigs and tore tail-feathers as it passed. This civil-
ian atrocity, often perpetrated, soon teaches hawks
to be more than wary. She had heard trunk-tap-
pings at the further side of the woods, and had
furtively swung up there to await developments.
She is less discreet when her clutch is older, even
refusing to fly at all until the invader is at her
very walls.

Dictates of common sense and caution had first
to be conquered; then it was up and up, around
and around, knot and branch, wrist and spur, hip
and thigh, until, at last, Ultima Thule. . . . Ah,
large eggs these two, fit for trophy room; worthily hawked at, worthily gained; they should have
a place of honor in the records!—And no one the
loser. No. For in another month at longest,
Mother Red-tail would again bring forth more
rufous globules—and the circle of life go on un-
checked. Tell me, fox chasers, lion shooters, deer
stalkers, can Nature as soon repair your bloody
havoc? In a season?—Not in two. Hawking could

not offend a Hindu Swami of the Seventh Estate.

To catalogue the Fowler's adventures that day; woodlot after woodlot strung along the northern New York countryside; nest after nest discovered and looked into; leagues tramped, before the sunset brought sweet exhaustion; would be something too much of a tale to unfold to America's busy ears. The writer has desired to speak of that day's Hawking so that the wise encyclopedias be refuted—not that he might spin a Hawking Odyssey. Not a hunter's tale or fisher's yarn, braggart of slaughter, dripping with grim detail, so that by proxy you who read may be in at the death and receive a red brush out of every quarry. . . . So he is done.

The Fowler is singing a swan-song of his kind. Years back there were others of us: much correspondence used to pass between us in many states. Is he, now, a last Mohican uttering a barbaric yawp over the graves of his tribe? Where are they, that tribe?—where in the lands of Powhatan, Wachusett and Brandt? Alas, like the G.A.R., the thin white line of their ranks yearly has grown thinner and thinner. . . . If any yet hear my voice, I beseech you, brethren, hawk while you may, for the era of oil is come upon you unawares. Be not cast down, for as long as you survive,

Hawking will not be obsolete nor the motor car the one god of Zion.

To others: unto this Lost Cause, unto this Barren Land, unto this inland Atlantis, the Fowler can but repeat Robert Frost's naïve invitation:

"I shan't be gone long—you come, too!"

It Just Isn't So

"Look out, it may be poison!" "Careful, now, he might bite you!" How many times have I heard such cautions uttered by grown-ups when I have been accompanying groups on countryside walks hereabout! It is exasperating. Instead of being necessary, this perpetual attitude tends to implant and perpetuate silly fears—fears which over-shadow the wonders of nature with a grim antagonism not there at all.

Take the matter of snakes. There *are* a few Copperheads outside the boundaries of Appalachian fastnesses, and there *are* certain rocky rough areas above Mason-Dixon's Line where the northern Rattlesnake can be located by searchers. But there are, north of Maryland, probably no places where nature-lovers might stray and encounter a single Cotton-mouth or Water Moccasin. Now, I have been a hiker, camper, hunter and nature enthusiast since I was six, and *never* have I run across a poisonous snake outdoors! That is, nowhere throughout the North. (Of the southern states I say nothing here, for I have seen both

Rattlers and Coral Snakes down there, and once a Copperhead.) Had they been distributed through this section; had they been a reasonably common menace that should cause a person to watch his step and mind his bed-site; surely I would have met at least *one*. On the other hand, never having been foolishly scared and made super-cautious, I have become acquainted with all the harmless snakes in this region, and enjoyed nature experiences galore with all manner of wild life.

For which I am profoundly thankful! I believe it safe to assert that more danger lies lurking in the omnipresent ice cream cones of the land than in the entire reptile population. (Vital statistics prove milk bacteria more of a menace than snake venom.) To avoid the one-in-a-million chance of snake-bite, I would not keep my children out of thicket, tangle and marsh, and cause them to forego a host of joys there which are their birthright! Recourse to a standard work on snakes will teach a person to recognize the aforesaid trio; to know their haunts; and how wisely to avoid careless intimacy.

Rattlesnakes, you will discover, do not *always* shake you a warning; nor are they the only snakes whose tail-tips tremble violently against surrounding vegetation when excited, although the others possess no rattles. Belief in the unfailing gallantry of Rattlers must go.

Another canard is ripe for decease: that Milk-snakes milk cows. They never do! And that there is such a thing as a Hoop-snake who when startled will seize its tail and roll swiftly down hill—positively, "there ain't no sech animal!" And again, that all snakes "bite." . . . Milk-snakes, Puff Adders, Water Snakes and Black Snakes—the most common of our harmless snakes—can be handled by using first a long stick with a short fork at the end to pin down the neck just behind the head, while you take a firm grip at the same place and another at the middle of the body. Occasionally, a large specimen, if not so held by the stick, can inflict a superficial bite on your hand; otherwise you could dispense with the aid and pick him up directly.

Stampede is not called for the moment you see a Skunk or sniff one in the offing. Except as a last resort, one will not discharge his scent. He much prefers wandering guilelessly off about his business than to go looking for trouble. Stand and watch him: observe the sort of food he spends his nights seeking: then perhaps you will be ready to believe that Skunks are not the relentless enemy of poultry they are generally thought to be—for such is the truth.

One misapprehension which keeps a lot of people from having more fun in the out-of-doors is held by city folks who have come to understand that wild-life and its haunts have disappeared near suburbs and towns. Not so—one who has the knack of it will discover an astonishing amount of wild activity almost at his very doors. I assure you of this, for I have repeatedly, and in many states, demonstrated its reality. Even a neglected spot of a few acres is sure to be harboring more than meets the casual eye. Remember that the motorist sticks to his concrete and cushions, as a general thing, and passes blindly scores of coverts he little dreams lie close beside the road. Automobiling has, in fact, hardly disturbed Nature at all.

But to resume being specific: You may have been as credulous as I was, when a small boy, so that you did put a horse-hair—a long one from the tail—into a bottle of water and wait for it to turn into a snake. This hoax is met so frequently of late that I know it to be still going strong. . . . Sometimes, after one has grown up, he forgets that a number of such stories are making their rounds of the newer generation—only to have them crop up blithely when he overhears children at play. Now, you would scarcely credit the longevity of the absurd legend about the slaughtered snake's tail "not dying until sunset," unless you hear it twenty years after you had forgotten it. Nor could you imagine the perennial occurrence of a so-called "sixth sense" which warns some people of the proximity of an unseen snake; except that you still have stories related to you by otherwise sensible adults.

"Oh, yes, handling a toad gives you warts!" positively asserts nearly every child, and I have met a half-dozen grown-ups who will not have it otherwise. Probably because a toad's skin looks "warty," the connection was once made, and the date of its making actually goes back into remote antiquity. Nothing to it at all. No more than there is in the recipe for banishing warts by washing your hands in a rain-water pool in a rock-hollow —at the full-moon! I was told of this cure for my own graceless school-boy hands by several country wives of my acquaintance. I feel sure the process is still being recommended in these parts. Smile, if you will—but such things are common "knowledge"!

The Candlemas Day legend about the ground-hog's shadow—it gets newspaper space every February—despite the fact that north of latitude 42 degrees, February 2nd is almost inevitably followed by six and eight weeks of "winter," and despite the utter emptiness of any theory as to meteorological knowledge on the part of a wood-chuck. As long as the myth is regarded as a pleas-antry, no fault can be found. But you will easily discover a minority who still treat it as fact. These same people probably belong to the Goose-bone School of weather forecasting. To predict whether the coming winter will be mild or rigorous, they tell you, all you need do is watchfully to study the condition of a young goose's wish-bone, or how high the muskrats thatch their lodges, or how plentiful the autumn nut crop is. Several careful check-ups on these rural theories have demolished them for all time—that is, in scientific circles. I remember once listening in at the country store while a hot debate raged as to whether a large area of soft cartilage on the goose breast-bone meant an "open" winter, or whether in fact it prophesied a hard one. When experts differ so fundamentally, it is difficult for a mere layman to take sides.

Going back to actual dangers for a moment: I suppose there are fewer than ten things which could be so classed in the northeastern quarter of these states. Learn to know Poison Ivy and Poison Sumach; don't handle Nettle unless you want to be in for a prickly fifteen minutes; play safe with

the jaws of an old Snapping Turtle; avoid eating
Baneberry and Nightshade berries—you wouldn't
anyway, for they are painted in "warning colors";
distinguish the two poisonous Aminita Toadstools
from all the edible ones; keep away from deer-
hunters' guns in the open season;—and the expectation of a long and happy life is greater in
the country than on city streets. The fatal cases
of snake-bite per annum are absolutely negligible.

I discovered this gem of utter falsehood not
long ago in a small city's newspaper. It was from
a "canned editorial"—that is, cheap syndicated
matter as supplied to hundreds of American papers
in small cities and towns.

> Another important poisonous plant is snakeroot.
> Whole settlements have been wiped out by the disease
> caused by this weed. For years people called the fatal
> sickness swamp fever or ague, and believed it came
> from the water, soil, evil mists, or miasma. Within the
> past two years, however, scientists have discovered that
> snakeroot causes this swamp fever. Snakeroot is eaten
> by cows and the poison is dissolved in their milk. Men
> drink this milk, are stricken with "milk sickness" and
> die.

Dear, dear! Since there are three plants called
snakeroot, it is uncertain which is referred to; and
since the country is full of "scientists," the discov-

erers of this malignant vegetable will probably
never be known.

How many times have you heard the "Nightingale" sentimentally referred to in popular songs
and poetry as if it were an American bird? Innumerable times, no doubt. But there are no Night-
ingales this side of the Atlantic and never have
been. How often have you heard about the honey
in flowers? Honey does not occur in any flowers.
Honey is a heavenly liquid manufactured in the
stomachs of bees, intended by Nature as a food for
the bee's larval young and for sustenance in the
hive during winter. Nectar is produced by many
flowers, a sweetish fluid whose function is to attract insects and hummingbirds so that these may
accomplish cross-fertilization by bringing pollen
from bloom to bloom. That honey is the most
delectable sweet in the world, almost instantly
digestible by human beings, certainly by compari-
son casts no reflection upon the variously scented
nectars which are its main source; nor upon a bee's
internal machinery!

City living is not conducive to moon-gazing,
but if it were it may be doubted whether the average gazer would master to his satisfaction the
varying shapes and moods it goes through during
the year. Ruralists have been free to study moon

phases since the days of Babylon, yet you will hear
them often sagely discussing whether the current
orb up there is a "wet moon" or a "dry moon."
"If the old Indian can hang his powder-horn on
the lower tip," they say, "we are in for a dry
spell." As a matter of fact, the crescent tips slightly
back and forth according to the season of the year
and the length of time since it was last full. Planting such things as cucumbers, rye and potatoes "in
the dark of the moon" is a persisting superstition
you will meet in many places in New England.

Notwithstanding that no Equinoctial storm
really takes place, there is still a persistent mode
of foretelling weather by certain peculiarities of
the so-called line storm. Drop in at the village
post-office some autumn evening and you will
surely hear all about it. As for the peach-twig theory of locating underground water supplies, this is
the Methuselah of them all! That a forked twig
held gingerly by both hands—hands, by the way,
of a proved "water-finder" only—will bend down
slightly when carried over the spot where it is wise
to sink a well, is one of the most widely believed
nature-fakes. Like the fable of swallows *hibernating in mud*, the peach-twig delusion stays ever
with us.

Will a bird desert her eggs if one of them be

touched by human fingers? Very rarely. I have encountered only two cases in thirty years of bird-nesting—and even these might have been due to an accident to the parent. A Nighthawk and a Whip-poor-will usually *moves* its pair of eggs if the nest spot is discovered; a Woodcock will some-times transport or load its tiny young from the vicinity of its revealed nest; a mother Rabbit will carry her hairless brood to a new fur-lined hiding place; these clever dodges I have known of. But I doubt that a taint of hands can linger on an egg-shell strongly enough to over-rule a bird's love of home.

One of the things regularly pointed out as "poison!"—and children seem universally to be-lieve it—is "frogspit." Now, frogspit isn't what its name applies at all. You see little chunks of froth on grass stems, weeds, tree twigs. Well, these are one of the many marvelous adaptations of insects, being liquid smoke-screens, so to speak; a liquid exuded from the abdomen of little hop-pers (the Spittal Insects) and whipped into a foamy cloud a hundred times the size of the crea-ture, to hide it from enemy eyes. Not only is it non-poisonous, but it is not even irritating to skin or tongue. Another insect is in undeserved bad odor: the Dragon Fly. "Darning-needles" they

are popularly called. By mentally transforming
the word "darning-needle" (derived from its long
slender shape) into fancied application as a sewing
instrument, our ancestors somehow arrived at the
concept that Dragon Flies will "sew up your ears."
"Look out for him—don't let him light on you!"
shrieks the country visitor. Transferring the fear
a little further removed from reality, perpetually
fearful folk tell you that these insects are particularly dangerous to the ears of horses and cows!

"I don't believe that many grown-ups take all
such things seriously," some of my friends have
retorted. "Very likely children do; but after we
get older, we know better than to be taken in by
these self-evident bits of hokum." To which I am
obliged to protest: "Ah, well, perhaps *you* do,
having done some reading on the subject and
given it considerable thought. But too many fearful visitors come up this way whose interest in the
out-of-doors is recent, asking me to take them
around a bit; too many charming misapprehen-
sions keep bobbing up in the course of a ramble;
to make me feel you are right. Honestly, now,
have you punctured them *all*, these myths I have
been exposing,—every one of them?"

"Do you, for instance," I launch out, "think
that most spiders sting or bite? Do you not regard

newts and salamanders as *lizards?* Don't you call
poisonous fungi toadstools? Hadn't you believed
that all large hawks are "hen hawks," preying on
poultry, and might well be shot on sight? Your
cat at home—I'll wager you consider cats as harmless, lovable animals, gentle, artless and lazy.
Some cats are, of course—in the towns and in the
daytime. But pussy is by nature a night animal
and her daylight habits are deceptive. Do you not
realize that where she can, she is a terror to birds,
chipmunks, rabbits and squirrels, as well as rats
and mice; no matter what a cozy, stretchy, cuddly
bunch of fur she may be around the house? One
suburban cat is reported as having killed over five
hundred birds in one season! One of my neighbor's cats destroyed five groups of nestlings on
my property this season. Are you sure that Hummingbirds never alight except at the nest? Do
you know a "weed" from a "plant"; a fruit from
a vegetable? Haven't you credited newspaper reports about baby toads raining down from the
sky in myriads? Did you know that a Black Squirrel was not a separate species, but only a color
phase of the Gray, just as red-headed folks are
merely "freaks" or "sports" of the human blonde?
Did you also happen to be aware that Black Bears,
Woodchucks, Screech Owls, sheep, and a few other

creatures also produce these dark members occasionally? Are you able to deflate many a first Spring Robin controversy by remarking that Robins frequently reside north of New Jersey all winter? Will you contend that earthworms cannot *feel?*" By this time I am breathless but usually I have won my point.

You may feebly subside with—"well, *what of it?*" To this I have no comeback. If you haven't much interest in nature-lore, anyway, why you wouldn't have read this far! Surely there is provocative material enough in these paragraphs to set you thinking. Perhaps they have warmed you into a desire to look closer into the fascinating world of plant and animal life. With this kindly hope, I present you one more fallacy as a conclusion. . . .

Bats share with rats, mice and English Sparrows, the distinction of being about the only warm-blooded untamed creatures which can be observed in a city. Seemingly something dramatic *had* to be invented about bats! Being utterly aloof from human affairs and utterly harmless, it would never do to let these witch-attendants off without attributing some low characteristic to them. Why this vindictiveness crops out in otherwise sensible people when they meet a strange wild animal, I

have no idea. . . . At any rate, the story goes
that bats try to fly into your hair; not only to snarl
it and tweak it, but to leave vermin there. I'll
wager that every one of my readers has heard this
one! . . . The slander very likely goes away
back into the voodooism of pre-Christian Europe
—surely it is time we stopped repeating it to our
children. Bats are not "birds," either, as is all too
commonly supposed. They form a family of mammals, not distantly linked with the mice clan.
Catch one daylighting behind your blinds, or
moping in your dark attic, or hanging in a hollow
tree, and study him. His pliable soft-skinned
wings are a marvel; his almost vestigial eyes hard
to find; his odd mouth equipment singularly interesting. Another phenomenon you will not dis-
cern with your own eyes is his ability to *fly by
sound*. We think it wonderful that an aviator nowadays is able to fly his machine "blind"—that is,
without seeing where he is going. Bats millenniums ago accomplished this! The hairs on an area
of the forehead are so sensitive that blindfolded
bats can flutter about in a cage criss-crossed with
threads, and not hit one of them! It is concluded
that the reflection of the wing-beat sound comes
vibrating back to its ears from any kind of an ob-
stacle before them. When such things are won-

dered about and observed from the squeaking little fellow in your hand, you will probably be glad it found a place "under your hair" rather than in it.

I have picked out at random a few of the commoner fallacies in the nature realm. A volume could readily be compiled to discuss them all. (Some day I hope to complete such a book.) If they were not widely credited among grown-ups, how is it that they get passed down from generation to generation? Youngsters do not get them out of the air. It is true that children make up a host of charming fables; but these I have been presenting are standbys whose uniformity indicates a perennial and fecund source "higher up."

My only plea is that the fears engendered by many of them be routed by common sense and a general skepticism, so that wide-awake children will be enabled to have more fun in the world outside the door. . . . Of course, the final way to tell fable and fact apart is by making your own first-hand studies of all the stories you hear—in print and out—for the *fiction* you hear is no stranger, no more intriguing, than the *truth* you will discover. But *discovering*—by inducting yourself into nature-study—that means a wider and keener interest on your part. . . . And this is the purpose I had in mind when I began this chapter.

A Practical Disarmament
Achievement

In these somewhat topsy-turvy times during which so much history is being re-written, figures of supposed contemptible reputation are being provided with so many laudable characteristics, and once admirable personages are being so searchingly criticized, that we hardly know where we stand. Now, a most unsavory item in natural history has come into his own. Not a deceased item, by any means. The Skunk, it is he to whom I refer, is very much alive today, and very much with us out here where the grass begins. In fact, probably, more with us than ever before, both in a wild and a domesticated state. Skunks, like rabbits, raccoons, deer and 'possums, are finding the greatly expanding areas of deserted farm-land highly to their liking. All over the east, at least, erstwhile pastures, meadows and fields are becoming thicket and woods, and the wild creatures naturally take advantage of the farmers' defeat.

The Skunk is being studied and known for what he truly is: both an economic asset and an esthetic pet. Up around these parts of northern New York he is now let alone and spared where once he was persecuted; and not because of his over-notorious faculty of enforcing aloofness, but because of his value. Of course, I allude to the treatment he gets from May to October, and not what befalls him after cold weather sets in and his summer coat becomes fur. I can well remember the days when the sight of a Skunk made the farmer see red. Nay, when even a faint scent of him was sure to bring outdoors the shotgun and the dog. Our ruralists had chickens uppermost in their minds at such times—and henhouse eggs, too. Things have changed somewhat to the animal's advantage.

Not, however, entirely to his advantage—for he still carries wrapped loosely around his flabby winter figure one of the finest pelts in these United States. To an extent likely to astonish people who are not conversant with some of the newer trends in farming, Skunks are being raised as an "agricultural product" in ever-increasing herds—or is it "studs"? Statistics showed a few years back that theirs was the most valuable hand-grown fur crop the country produced—and, I have no doubt, is easily more so now, as Skunk-farms are more numerous. There is even a Skunk Fancier's Journal published for circulation among the trade! I have before me a volume entitled *Skunk Raising for Profit*, from which I, at any rate, have profited—in the realm of nature-lore if not financially. Our busy Department of Agriculture also has found time to issue an authoritative pamphlet upon a similar topic. From these I have gleaned a lot of information on *disarmament*—that is what they call it "officially". Things I had not known before, after a life-time of more or less intimate contact with the interesting creatures up here near the Adirondacks, come tumbling from these scientific pages. Even the word *disarmament* is a new term to me, and one, I submit, which is as deft as it is scientific. We used to call the not unknown process "removing the scent glands"—and I humbly admit that the present operation is simplicity itself compared with the crude old-fashioned one.

This charming word *disarmament* is equalled in aptness by the new name for the animal itself, which is not only proposed for public use, but is commonly employed in the literature of the modern industry. The new cognomen—and one in much better odor, so to speak, with all who talk purposefully on the subject—is Sachet Kitten. I tried this name out on an old-time trapper and hunter in these parts last week, but as he only wrinkled his forehead in perplexity to make out what I was driving at, I judge there is still considerable propaganda work in front of the movement. Surely it is not as Sachet Kitten that it has provided in recent years one-fourth of all the pelts marketed in America.

I do not intend to devote much of this scripture in praise of the Skunk to mere economic and surgical facts, but to the ways and means by which he has endeared himself to me as a denizen of the wilds and as a pet. But since I have introduced so much already under the former heads, I may as well set down a few more paragraphs.

There is little doubt but that Skunks would merit the personal attention they deserve if only they could live down whatever's in a name. "Skunk" is short and ugly. Moreover, it has long borne application to certain sorts of human beings, as well. But, call them Sachet Kittens, and a new future looms before them. Sachet Kitten it will be, sooner or later. Have not inspired breeders in solemn convention so decreed? They have. Not unnaturally they feel resentful that their loved fur has been outrageously slurred by being incredibly processed and made up under alien names. It is offered for final sale as a product of half-a-hundred wholly mythical creatures, the most common misnomers being Civet Cat and Alaska Sable.

I have seen it as Chinese Otter and Wood Mink! These countless aliases have been resorted to to avoid calling a Skunk a Skunk. It is high time the furriers themselves began making our wives and daughters "skunk-minded," educating them to the real standards of excellence concealed beneath that rugged coat! . . . Wood Mink, indeed!

Most of us are naturally sympathetic with that jaded gourmet who sighed—"Oh, for a *new* animal!" Many of us have expressed the same wish. But as pet-lovers and not as gourmets. Now, it appears from the aforesaid publications, we are offered a new pet. I heartily accept the offer. Long before the fact appeared in print, we up-state boys were aware of it, and some of us made practical application of the knowledge. Yet, somehow, the fad has not prospered. Dogs and cats—or even tiger-cubs, for that matter—properly trained, have free entrée into the most effete society. The Skunk has not. Why? The answer seems obvious —*is* obvious. That is, unless we have read up on disarmament.

It is not generally known that, bereft of its sole defensive weapon—and it has no weapons of offense!—*Mephitis putida* is not at all mephitic; but on the contrary, is the most *ideal* of pets. Likewise, it is not public knowledge how simple a matter it is to disarm him. (And, of course, *her*.) A slight operation does not take an accustomed hand five minutes and is not actually as severe as the common spaying process done upon female dogs and cats. Removal of the two tiny scent-glands at the base of the tail, preferably before the animals are two months old, is the invariable detail of practice on all American Skunk-farms. (Be it remarked that the glands have nothing to do with sex-functions.) Thus disarmed, there remains no reason why they should not be received with open arms in any household. And, as a matter of proud record to fanciers, they *are* thus being adopted rather commonly through the Middle West.

The possession of claws, capable on occasions of necessity in the wild state of inflicting real injury on its enemies, does not endanger the cat's place in the world of pets; nor should it the similarly endowed Mephitis. We do not hold it against dogs that canine teeth are, if misdirected, a menace even to human life. Neither the teeth nor claws of our striped wood-pussy can compete with those of dogs and cats. But its ingratiating qualities can.

On several occasions I have watched both old and young de-natured Skunks, home-raised and home-wonted, being vigorously played with by children. As much fun on one side as the other!

They actually enjoyed the human company, just as dogs would. The plumey tails of the sleek animals were as expressive of fun and vivacity as the faces and shouts of the youngsters.

Since the writer has never personally owned a fully domesticated pet Skunk, he must present his final endorsement of the new movement in the words of two prominent scientists who have. Dr. C. Hart Merriam, the well-known naturalist, pays this tribute: "These animals, particularly when young, make very pretty pets; being attractive in appearance, gentle in disposition, interesting in manners, cleanly in habits—rare qualities, indeed. They are playful, sometimes mischievous, and manifest considerable affection for those who care for them. I have had at different times ten skunks in confinement. From some of them I removed the scent glands. But the greater number were left in a state of nature. One of these was particularly companionable. While I drove about the country he would sleep in my pocket. He was very frolicsome and playful." Mr. Cory, the Curator of Zoology at Field Museum, Chicago, says: "Naturally of an affectionate disposition, he will rival cat or dog for your favors, and children can play with him at will. . . . Disarming in no way affects his health or happiness."

So far as my observations of wild Skunks go, their own domestic housekeeping is above reproach. Victims of an immemorial slander, the stern truth is that they are admirable exemplifiers of minding one's own business; never known to provoke an attack of chemical warfare nor to fire until fired upon. They are as nonbelligerent as Molly Cottontail, and they are certainly not as destructive to wild birds as roaming tame cats. They are omnivorous as to food—which means that their diet is as wide as the woods: vegetables, meat scraps, beetles, grasshoppers, moles and shrews, eggs, earthworms, cut-worms in the sod and in captivity, bread-and-milk, chicken-feed, etc. As mousers, they can outdo the average feline. I have never seen the fact stated, but can state it here on my own authority that at times they feed heavily on ants. Last spring, I happened to be able to watch one through my binoculars at work on an ant-hill mound in a thicket. He had already dug off the entire top of the mound and was busily gobbling up the big black ants. During the next few weeks I found numerous other ant-hills so flattened off—in fact, most of them I ran across had thus been treated. But this phenomenon was new to me, and I suppose only occasional food shortages force them into such straits. February and early spring are the only time during which they can be truly said to be a danger to farmers' poultry and eggs. At other times, their own natural food suffices.

There is honor among Skunks. One recent May evening as I was walking across a wide upland pasture, I saw a large "full-stripe" digging little pockets in the sod after white grubs—as they commonly do. After watching him finish making and exploring four of them, I approached nearer. When he saw me he erected his plume, quivered its tip vigorously, and raised his head. Being in plain sight, the six-foot man-object standing there apparently promised no ill towards him, and presently he went on working. I rolled a round stone his way. Again he stopped and mildly warned me with his tail. Another round stone, and he moved off slowly in the opposite direction. Desiring to prove his pacificism more thoroughly, I went rapidly towards him. Although the Skunk did not go any faster, he had evidently recognized a pest. At intervals he would pause and wave to me; finally executing a series of little up and down jumps with his fore feet. He patted the ground sharply as if to call attention to his presence and request me to stop coming on my particular course. But I tossed a pebble at him—and then he knew he was in for it. No more running; now he planted himself and patted the turf in earnest! "Can't say I didn't warn you!" he indicated. "Now watch out!" Twenty feet away I intelligently stopped. We faced one another for perhaps five whole minutes. Then, with slow dignity, he crossed over to a fence hedgerow and lost himself in the dusk. Now what could have been more honorable?

Only rarely will you see one in daylight between six and six, for a Skunk is nocturnal. To see a sedate file of youngsters being led forth in the evening dew is a common but intriguing sight. Then the mother is much less inclined to stand for intrusions. In fact, I have had the parent start directly towards me without hesitation.

City-bred people almost invariably run the moment they see a Skunk in the offing—just as they do when they happen upon any kind of a snake. This is a foolish thing to do, and quite needless. If one has any hankering for nature experiences, he can get a pack of enjoyment from observing the beautiful black and white creatures.

The Skunk is one of the weasel clan. All the weasels—minks, ferrets, ermine, badgers, otters—have defensive scent-glands, and their flesh seems purposely unpalatable to enemies. The Skunk, only, is able to throw that offensive odor by muscular contraction. He does not "throw it with his tail" as is commonly supposed; that adornment serves as a signal. But without its erection over the back, the muscles at its base cannot operate. Any of our country boys know that you may carry a Skunk home by the end of his tail in perfect safety. You will, however, never be able to get hold of that tail on a wild animal, except when you have dug one out from its winter hibernation. The scent is thrown *backward* and can be shot up out of a burrow into a dog's face while the burrower is working himself in. You may *face-to-face* a Skunk with equanimity—if he will permit it. Experienced dogs know this, and in the open will manœuver to pounce head-on. Such dogs are also aware that odor is not the only quality of this chemical. Odor is the least thing a dog would resent. But the fluid has a highly irritating effect on eyes or exposed mucous membrane surfaces; it is burning and blinding. Without doubt, in a state of nature, the scent is merely to provide a lasting association with the tear-gas power possessed by the liquid itself, and to cause enemies to pass by on the other side.

Because they are of the weasel clan, Skunks are forever nosing about in dark corners, inquisitive, investigative, alert, thorough in their hunting; but

never fidgety or nervous. I have never known one
to show fear. Diligently and persistently, they will
fatten themselves up in the autumn, to retire in
November for a three-month hibernation. They
do not invariably hibernate—especially south of
the Erie Canal latitude. Up here where winter
demands that fur be fur, and not merely hair, you
do not see the dainty tracks in the snow until crust-
forming time. Along in February they begin coming out of their holes and journeying long dis-
tances for a chance meal. It is now that nearby hen
roosts should be tight shut at sunset. I remember
following one track from my barns for three miles
until I reached a spot where lay the scattered remains of one of my White Leghorns. The ma-
rauder had actually dragged and carried the hen
all that distance! A half-mile further was the hole
into which he had retired. Unlike woodchucks,
Skunks do not prefer to hibernate alone. Often a
whole family stay together a year, and even a
miscellaneous collection of unrelated animals will
den in for the winter. A friend once dug out nine
Skunks from one hole, all adults with various
styles of marking, and later trapped two more belated lodgers who were trying to enter at the other
entrance to the den—it having been a home ex-
cavated by woodchucks who invariably construct

two doorways. His check for the pelts was, even in those dollar-a-day days, something we lads talked about for years! Through a bedroom window we used to watch a completely black Skunk come nightly to our garbage pail and vainly endeavor to lift off the lid. Every once in a while we purposely left the cover off—just to encourage his visits. Of late years, it seems as though they do far less prowling about the premises; probably because ours and our neighbors' acres are woods where in father's time they were corn and oat fields.

There is considerable variation in markings. And, inexplicably enough, the less white on them, the finer the quality of the fur. Pelts running heavily to white bring a low market figure. Fur dye being what it is today, white stripes would not matter, except for the fact that the texture of the hairs is coarser. Protective coloration explains well enough the value of black and white as a night-time camouflage, but it does not account for the difference in fibre.

Motorists are taking heavy toll of our Skunks. They *need* every member of their large families. Not used to getting rapidly out of the way of anything, they get run over in thousands. Not one automobile driver, with whom I have talked about it, will avoid hitting one if he can. Now, this is too bad! They are protected by closed seasons in most states, but for motor cars there is no closed season. Seldom do you notice much odor when you come upon a carcass on the road, and that is because the little animal simply did not know what had hit him!

One day last September I drove fifty miles along a concrete highway closely paralleling the northern boundary of New Jersey. It was at the end of the month, and we had had our first stiff frosts. In that fifty miles I counted the crushed pelts of five Skunks. When I returned home I took a pencil and did some figuring. Assuming that the official statistics are correct, there are almost exactly 111,200 miles of improved highway in New York State. Fifty miles goes into that total 2,224 times; multiply the latter by five Skunks, and you reach the amazing probability that around eleven thousand of the animals died on highways in the space of a few days. Reasoning further that the tangible flesh and blood record of casualties remains in sight but three days, you could double that eleven thousand for a week's toll, and multiply the product by as many of the fifty-two weeks as you had the heart to. Then, if you proceed a bit further, you will think of all the *unimproved* roads in the state—and finally come out with an estimate of the annual motor mortality for Skunks, in one state alone, which simply staggers you! How on earth the species is able to increase its census, as apparently it is doing, in the face of the automobile, transcends my guessing power. Undoubtedly, we need considerable more statistics and knowledge about humble Mephitis, if we are to account for it.

Yes, the Skunk is having its record rewritten. He is being appreciated in many quarters—if not among motorists. Almost incredibly, he is "coming back," both racially and in reputation. Game wardens up here admit it; farmers deplore it. Little black and white wood-pussy may destroy pheasant and grouse eggs and chicks; and he may like his poultry where he finds it; but to nature-lovers and fur breeders alike he still yields rich dividends. As self-appointed spokesman for the naturalists, I welcome his renaissance!

Sic Transit

I HAVE recently made a discovery. It startles me. Looking off across the landscape panorama from my front-back porch, I suddenly realized that this family, of which I am—for income-tax purposes, at least—head, are truly *pioneers*. Now, one is accustomed to think of a pioneer family as going back in local antecedents for two or three generations. Yet twelve years is the span of our own tenure here. Human time, on the wings of airplane and the wheels of the motor-car, moves much faster of late.

Pioneers. Yes, even though family chattels include an internal-combustion carriage, instead of a Canastoga Wagon; and its real estate culminates in a steam-heated cottage, and not a moss-caulked cabin of logs. Should it be said that we *are*, or *were*, pioneers? Perhaps both. When we came, we were pioneers; now, abruptly recognizing that we are face to face with a new and different generation, a changed countryside, no doubt but that we are as people of an elder day; the "oldest inhabitants" in a milieu of modern suburban settlement.

When we came, it was, to us, a new country. To another migration since the World War, it is likewise a Land of Canaan.

Until yesterday it seemed sheer hyperbole to think of ourselves as of a breed with the first indomitables who toiled

Up along the hostile mountains
Where the hair-poised snowslide shivers—
Down and through the big fat marshes
That the virgin ore-bed stains;
'Til they heard the mile-wide mutterings
Of unimagined rivers,
And beyond the nameless timber saw illimitable plains!

Yet a certain kinship there is. The term "pioneer" has, after all, only a relative meaning. It has reference to the in-comer himself, not to the land to which he comes. There is egotism about the word. Nothing new under the sun but the newcomer who makes it so. "We do not discover; we forget," aptly said La Rochefoucauld. A hair divides the pioneer from the rear-guard. Where does a circle begin—and end? Who pioneered the Ohio Country and Missouri before the Mound Builders? Who tilled Britain's soil ere the Celts came? Was Eric the Red a pioneer in Labrador? Daniel Boone, John Sevier, George Rogers Clark, Joseph Smith: were they spoken of as pioneers in the tribal annals of the Sioux and the Shawnees? Where, save at the poles, has a pioneer gone unopposed or unwelcomed by men who once were pioneers themselves? And here, in New England, *we* suddenly find ourselves the last of the rustic Mohicans where so recently we must have come as intruders, too. Our commuting, summer-residing, sun-tanning neighbors hold us in splendid isolation, and we them.

While I mused yesterday on the porch overlooking four hundred acres of woodland, crumbling orchards, thicketing hill-pastures,—whose every chain-perch-and-rod, except our own, is in fee-simple to absentee city speculators, I was made aware of the resentment which an autocthonous people, the "original" inhabitants, feel at the intrusion of a lustier civilization. In a flash I understood why the Kentucky mountaineer moved "farther back"; why New England farmer and townsman do not receive as one of themselves the summer boarders and retired cityfolk who come among them; why the native son of Ozark and Adirondacks carps bitterly at a "progress" which brings the outsider impudently into their midst. And, standing there, we bethought ourself that now, twelve years after our own advent, we were pioneers; and, in a sense, vanguards of a horde that is now upon us.

Twelve years ago the highway half a mile distant was not topped by a floor of concrete, and the site of yonder police dog farm grew only butternuts, cow-parsnips and goldenrod. Where that haughty upstanding colonial mansion stares at us above the knolls was a hepatica-and-violet paved thicket, seamed by a hazel-shaded brook. Now there is a billboard or two on the aforesaid highway, and this week they are for the first time visible through the thinning leaves. And next year will put a score there. As we stood, a strange sound floated on the breeze: the faint whine of a steam saw which had just started upon the incredible profanity of cutting off the two-mile-deep woodlot beyond the billboards! Unbelievable that a twelvemonth from now those woods where, in the days of our settlement, barred owls nested and hooted throatily o' nights, will be a Real Estate Development! That over there where yearly the returning Red-tail hawks have circled and screamed April greetings, will soon be stumpage! Not even stumpage, for these also will be blasted out. That tangled seclusion which tempted Green Herons and Hooded Warblers once will soon lie defenceless to the summer sun—the first step toward improvement (!) of the land. We have witnessed the complete evolution of the Building Lot! Does all this sound bitter? Rather, it is set down in sadness.

Such feelings as were ours, while we stood on the porch listening in sinking-hearted contemplation, must have been those of the pioneer in all places and all ages when the main army caught up to them. . . . A golf course, country estates, garages, Dutch Colonial, Spanish *Colonial* houses, electric lighting, telephone wires, shops, a super-sophisticated hotel—these are not remote possibilities but terrible probabilities. And we are bound to see all this as a barbaric invasion. With the coming of a second pioneer, the first ceases to be. Like the fierce queen, only one pioneer can live in the hive of human progress—and be content. Where once grouse, fox and wild duck were daily encounters, and woodchucks bundled clumsily about in the clover; where we caught infant rabbits in our hands and surprised raccoons and 'possums nosing around in the dark; will arise a Newer Stone Age culture, the encampments of a new race.

"America's last frontier is going—is gone!" we sighed. . . . Then smiled at the thought of our own coming as having been settlement upon a

frontier. What of our own reception? The octa-
genarian on the adjoining farm to whom we still
pay final mortgage installments—whose grand-
father actually got his deed from the Pequots—
how did he regard us when we came to spy out the
Promising Land? As pioneers or as upstarts? Four
springs ago our garden-patch yielded two arrow
heads in an afternoon's hoeing. That very afternoon, turning our eyes upward, from bean and
tomato vines, we beheld the first flight of the first
American airmail service. "A pioneer effort" we
murmured in awe. Yet we forgot that the Pequots
had their message carriers, too. . . . Verily, a
pioneer is no venturer—he is a morning person in
an afternoon land!

A cycle of Cathay has come to end. We should
not be resentful. This home has served its purpose
well. From the back-front porch we have seen
many things pass, besides time. In a rural seclusion
we have lived intimately with forty-eight seasons
and a hundred weathers. We have "set watch by
night, as shepherds, over the flocks of the sky,"
marking the summer stars creep up through the
blue pastures until Orion has come with his dogs
for the hunting; then satiated by the chase, he has
led them elsewhere for feasting and rest. Through

our own eyes, we have understood why all northern folk-legends (indeed, all earthly religions)
have appointed each its own Christ-mass at the
time when the Golden God, relenting, begins re-
tracing his steps back from the south, bringing life
again to His creatures. We have bowed down to
the universal Spring god, Eostre, on that March
day when darkness and light match as twin windows in earth's Cathedral of The Resurrection.
Upon our acres have we fashioned a green shrine
and shaped thereon a graven image of Eostre—
which looks not unlike a spreading young spruce
tree tipped with buds, because that is exactly what
it is. For Easter is the deity of reborn life; the
deity of uplift, of hope, of fertilization, of procre-
ation, of life-out-of-the-tomb; a god

> Whose secret Presence, through Creation's veins
> Running quicksilver-like eludes your pains;
> Taking all shapes from Mah to Mahi; and
> They change and perish all—but He remains!

Shiva, Christ, Friga, Kwan-non, Astarte, Bud-
dha, Isis: men everywhere have made that god in
their own image. As the Sphinx, unexpectant symbol of unquenchable hope, faces east to watch the
ants of eternity come one by one from the yellow
granary, in the never-ending Scheherazade-tale
which is life; so we from our porch. Four thou-

sand dawns have said to us: "Let there be light!"
—and in our pride we have answered: "Lo, there
is light!" yet knowing how great is that darkness!
. . . Now we see a new star in the east. But it is
a gasoline trademark on yonder billboard—must
we pioneers also worship that?

I am sure that our infiltrating neighbors of the
New Race cannot understand the inner New England farmer. He is never verbal, shuns emotion,
yet at times he feels deeply. His is an environment, a setting, which urbanites will ever be
strangers to. I have come to love the passing New
England, and to wonder how the future will equal
its serenity and simplicity. From the midst of my
furrows at sunset I have become aware of the fierce
passion which is his and the peasant's of all times
for the soil. Hoe in hand, while the Wood Thrush
and Veery were singing their vespers, I too have
been that peasant bare-foot in the dirt, a lust of
land hunger filling me to trembling. That dis-
trust of cities and machines is somehow intuitive,
immemorial. That first-hand contact with sun,
shower and soil, that business with animals, that
close partnership with nature in conjuring food
from the dull earth, are employments that have
roots down into the prehistoric nomad and agri-

cultural stages of the species. They are elements in the brotherhood of the sub-conscious which make all the world's farmers kin.

"A lonely spot you have," visitors have been used to say. We think not. At any rate, not more alone than philosopher or messiah whose words are unheard by his time. A pioneer has loneliness as one of his dearest prerogatives. Like any other thrifty almoner of life, taking what luck alone-ness offers, he whittles a virtue out of it, and pro-ceeds to like what he gets quite as ardently as though he had got what he liked. Which, in fact, he has—perhaps. . . . Blessed is he who can never solve the riddle: Did you really *want* it? or do you really *like* it?

If ever we lapse into that state of visceral dis-quietude commonly called loneliness, we have but to look up at the hilltops off there to the south. On those hills stands Jordan's old haybarn, a square knick in the skyline. No companion struc-ture within a mile and a half. It *looks* lonely, too. Then we remember that on the contrary it is one of the newsiest spots in the county, even though human beings rarely visit it. As if all *news* (north, east, south, west) were of man's making! That barn is one built, as was the custom of our New

England forefathers, for sheltering the surplus of bumper hay crops. It stands at the heart of what once was spreading hayfields. The fathers paid more attention to the roof—shingles were cheaper then—than to the sidings; because the center aisle of the structure, between the two packed bays, wintered the haywagon, horserake and mowing machine. (Nowadays these are left outdoors to rust!) Eleven months of the year its sequestration was, humanly speaking, complete. For the wild creatures of the meadows, it served as a sort of community center. It was as full of life as a pioneer is of thoughts.

A trip there at any season never lacked interest and rarely failed of surprises. I was forever going up there out of sheer curiosity. Its roof was a landing station to all the aerial neighborhood. Within, back in the eave-recesses, bats hid, Screech Owls moped and mice built cozy lairs of chaff and feathers. Upon niches in the rafters were perched Barn Swallows' mud nests, and occasionally a Phœbe's moss-covered cup too. The Eave Swallows stayed outside in those dirt-and-saliva retorts they build, and some years made as many as twenty of them there. The hay, stored solidly away in two wide bays twenty feet deep, was likely to remain undisturbed several summers; so long that it sheltered a perfect maze of rat and mouse runways; one could always catch muffled squeaks deep in the labyrinth. Hence the inmates of a weasel den in a nearby stone wall had no food worries. Chipmunks and squirrels sought sanctuary in the hay also on occasion, though what they lived on, out there in the open fields, one could hardly guess. Under the floor came a third stratum of life: Woodchucks, Rabbits, Quail, Ruffed Grouse during severe weather, and one winter a luckless Red Fox,— luckless, for it proved to be his last den. One May a pair of Bluebirds, utilizing cannily a knothole through the siding, raised a brood in a pocket dented into the hay within. Often when one swung open a door, a family tabby, a mile or so from home, would slink felinely off, disturbed while policing the teeming mows for mice. Spiders spun thick swathing webs over the dusty hay until it was made to look as unmarketable and unnutritious as dried leaves. Up against one gable-end, a nook in perpetual gloom, regularly two pairs of Chimney Swifts glued their twig cups. They maintained passage through the opposite gable-end which had a small square hole cut in it. Only in one other similar spot have I ever known these little chimney-sweeps to build a home. What, I used to wonder, did they do before the days of barns and chimneys? I found the answer a few years ago, not twenty rods from the hay barn itself.

In tne centuries when chimneys were only the tips of teepees, and teepees were themselves passing scarce, there did somehow develop a bird exactly designed for dwelling in the chimney-pots of civilization. Perhaps a gifted prophet might have foretold the coming of the white man from reflecting upon the Swift. But, this specialized creature, which can never alight except to cling to a vertical surface, was a natural result of having taken up quarters in hollow trees, and was therefore sentenced forevermore to live there or in caves. Then, as though expected, along came chimneys and disused barns. The long narrow eggs, a shape demanded by her bobbin-shaped body, began to increase a thousandfold. Nowadays Swifts are one of our common birds. It was one of those hollow trunks, open at the top, near the Jordan barn, that revealed what their home life was like before Columbus. This big tree had a hole at its bottom large enough for a man to crawl inside and stand. Standing brought my head on a level with four or five annually occupied nests and the remnants of former years. Fifteen feet above was the broken-off top of the stump. Apparently crowded out, two pairs always have resorted to the barn for nesting. For weeks one could watch the colony snatch at twiglets of nearby dead trees for nesting material. These twigs dampened with the sort of sticky saliva (which makes Birds' Nest Soup so delectable when it is served you in Shanghai) fashion the shallow cups against the inner gable.

What cozy shelter that barn gave when an August thunderstorm broke over the country! Dashing torrents beat with little effect upon its shingles, and as one lay upon the dusty pungent softness, engaging creepings and rustlings were all about. In winter it was impossible to pass by from a hunting trip and not be seized with a desire to go and look within—just to see what you might chance on. Lacey mouse trails and larger rat tracks seamed the snow where it had sifted between the siding. Juncos and Tree Sparrows had footed the white surface all around the outside. Crows had investigated before we did. A fresh skunk trail almost certainly led in under one corner. Snug, in and under this refuge, many an animal endured through a winter of waiting.

A few years back when June haying was on and the Jordan meadows were all sweaty activity, there was yearly panic among the dwellers on

South Hill. It took the muster of all their courage to keep swallows and swifts carrying on business as usual during these alterations; the other denizens absconded from the whole vicinity, like husbands from housecleaning, until conditions resumed normalcy once more. . . .

Next week, they tell us, the old barn is to be torn down and a "Norman" cottage built upon its foundations. There will be less interesting news up there from now on.

"Get a radio and hear the world!" our city cousins urged last fall. "Bless you," we replied snugly, "we have another world to hear first." The outside world has been broadcasting for years and would interfere with the city stations. Without any tuning-in or hooking-up, we have from our front-back porch caught programs from four different owls: Saw-whet, Screech, Barred, and Horned owls, on their different frequencies, "get us" quite often. But we are speaking only from memory. Many stations which used to be on the air have closed down and departed.

We have heard fox barks, frog voices from a dozen species, peevish bickerings from moles and shrews under the sod, and snatches also from the razor-sharp shrilling of red bats, most of whose notes are too high in wave-length for human ears to catch. In this locality from May 1st until along in September, the noise made all day by insects is so loud that sometimes one cannot hear another's voice two yards away. It is astonishing that so accustomed do we become to this blanket of sound covering the earth that we do not notice it. We hear through it rather than above it. If you try to become conscious of its steadiness and depth, you get the sensation of standing in a busy factory. After a few minutes you long for shelter from this rushing wind of noise; for the acute realization of its volume produces something like physical pain. Coming back home from a long absence, I once dropped into the middle of a June evening—this was how I first noticed the phenomenon. I could hardly hear the conversation on the porch, though others noticed nothing unusual. They tuned their ears through it, an unconscious trick I had temporarily lost. This may be the reason why your city dweller sleeps so poorly during his first nights in the country. Short- and Long-antennaed Grasshoppers, Tree Locusts, crickets, bees, wasps, the flying beetles, Leopard Frogs, Pickerel Frogs, were all in voice at once. In the daytime, Vesper, Field, Grasshopper and Song Sparrows, contribute to that pulsating, smothering surf of sound. Of course, after the Katydids begin their unparlia-

mentary discussions, they produce another sort of
static entirely. The jungle of locust saplings, cat-
brier and blackberry vines behind the barn then
produces such a torrent of noise that one cannot
carry on a conversation beside it. Standing there of
an evening, the illusion is perfect of a tropical
jungle upon the banks of a cascading river. That
thicket patch is so impenetrable that without an
axe you cannot cross it, and at night you certainly
could not *hear* across it.

The words "tropical jungle" have always had
for me a peculiar fascination. I suppose it began
with reading the old master, Mayne Reid, and was
further fortified by *The Life of Livingstone* and
With Clive in India. At any rate, I grew up knowing exactly how a jungle must look, smell and
sound. Had I been set down suddenly in upper
Bengal or along the Amazon, I thought I would
feel at home and know what to do. Having quitted
the porch on several occasions to go out into India
and the Orient—merely, it proved, to find that
New England was much the more interesting—
these far-away jungles seemed curiously familiar
places.

That New England also has her jungles, struck
me forcibly while foraging for green grapes last
fall. As with so many things with which one has

been a neighbor all his life, the real significance of our own northern jungles hardly occurs to us. But in late August try to force your way across a semi-marshy strip of ground along a creek where soil conditions are favorable. You will have literally to hack your way through—as the Borneans and Ceylonese do. Blackberry canes alone nearly fix you. Tough-stemmed Goldenrod, lush Jewelweed, Ironweed, Joe-Pye and Ten-petal Sunflower; all higher than your head, furnish most of the obstruction, as well as the main color display of the impasse. Where also twists thickly among the stockade of stalks Dodder, Tearthumb, Oswego Tea and grape-vines, not to mention the wiry Smilax, the eager greenery is welded into an astonishing mass. And it is a gorgeous jungle, with colors in autumn fit to compare with tropic Bougainvillæa, Kapok and Flame-tree.

Stand there on a grass tussock and look about you! It is impossible to name and number all the wild plant life crowding about. Vervain, Hardhack, Hedge Nettle, Boneset, Vetch, Huckleberry, Alder, Aster, mingled in endless confusion with fifty other species of late blooming plants. I assure you there is nothing in the tropics surpassing it. Filling the lower interstices are thick Skunk Cabbage leaves overgrown as if by elephantiasis;

tough Brakes, Lobelia, Toothwort, a dozen varieties of grasses. You must ruthlessly smash, thrash
and tear an aisle if you wish to cross.

When one reflects that in April he walked across
at this spot with no more hindrance than wet feet;
that this entire jungle here is of *annual* growth;
he is astounded. In tropic jungle there are centuries of vegetable construction, humus as light and
thick as saw-dust, for a sun is always overhead.
But here, before the first snowfall, the lush five-
month wilderness will wither and sink to the
ground. A lavish process. If you think it wonderful that moose and elk each year grow an enormous set of horns, consider that here nature grows
ten thousand million times as much vegetable
horn which is to serve purpose half as long. Once
this vast annual cellulose layer was stored as coal.
Nowadays it probably is not. Certainly not even
peat is formed in such thickets because every two
or three years a thoroughgoing grass-fire sweeps
through. We have on several occasions thought
ourselves lucky to save our buildings from con-
flagration,—only to find in the end that the more
certain flame of motor gasoline is bound to con-
sume them. Our homestead, like all the others
hereabout, can be had for a price—but in our case
we pay the price, a penalty every pioneer is heir to.

Our twelve years of "looking off across" (quaint phrase of our fathers'!) are at end. We shall sell out presently to the Building Stone Age. Having in past "mercenary interludes" made seven long journeys to the far corners of the globe, we know erstwhile New England to be the most beautiful and interesting region on it. Of this we harbor no doubts.

We shall depart with mingled sadness and satisfaction. We must not wait for an ending here like that of our predecessor. He who built this porch and built it on the "wrong" side of the house, knew which was the right side. He may have built better mousetraps than we can buy today, thinking that the world would make a path to his door in the end—which, alas, it did! The path worn by the guests at his funeral and the bidders at the subsequent auction. As one of the latter, we are sure he builded better than he knew; that even as he elected for a space to supervise the world from his porch, so he was elected at last, we hope, to be Supervisor of Outlooks in some new Land of Canaan. For us, in turn, there must be a "farther back," some retreat where police-dogs do not howl nor steam-saws whine. A place in whose "improvement" they plant trees rather than cut them. Per-

haps there we may become pioneers again! . . .
Salutamus Cæsar!

Yet, after all, why ascribe these changes, these
evolutions, these pioneer feelings, solely to New
England? Our land—all the world—is transforming under the incantations of steam and oil.
Wherever they sing in whirring wheels, humming
turbines, purring gears; keeping time to the
rhythmic beat of cylinders and throb of pistons;
backward retreats Nature, baulked and puzzled.
Is hers but a "strategic retirement to a stronger
position," or is it her defeat?

We cannot conceive of Nature defeated. "The
mechanical whirl-and-hurry world of the modern
city is illusory. All seem to hasten with it, accept
its tempo, speed with it down the ringing grooves
of industrialism. So in appearance, but not in reality. For the tempo of life is not life itself which it
hurries on through noise and change. The speedy,
the active ones seem to be the stream itself, but are
only its wavelets. Behind faces conformable to the
haste of modern experience are still philosophic
minds, contemplative, meditative, skeptical of
their own haste, brooding when they can. . . .
More daily is undertaken though not much more
worth counting is done. There is no better solu-

tion to the problem than Joshua's, who begged the sun to stand still while he finished his job at leisure; and, unlike him, we can expect no miracle. The busy world will go faster until it goes slower —though we shall not tarry here until the turn." *

Time is long and Nature has not been fleeting. The Egyptian-style in one great world era—four or five millenniums!—appeared to be the pattern of the universe; the *pax romanorum* seemed forever—longer than man's knowledge of the New World. (Someone has voiced his wonder at whether Cicero, standing at a corner of the Forum, could have dreamed of what twenty centuries have brought!) Our hands and thoughts may have changed, but our feelings are one with Ninevah and Tyre. Sunlight propels chlorophyl to feed the earth as it did in Sumeria; babies are yet born as Genghis Khan was born. Such fundamentals are an earnest of the future ahead of the race.

The triumph (!) of machines, the epoch of cities—shall men serve these two forever? This, in a last analysis, is the query which every nature-lover and peasant-heart refuses to answer: "Alas, yes!"

* From an editorial in the *Saturday Review of Literature*, April 6, 1929.

Part Four

BOOKS FOR IDENTIFICATIONS

Books for Identifications

*Fieldbook of North American Mammals. Anthony. Putnam.

Life of Animals. Ingersoll. Macmillan.

The Pet Book. A. B. Comstock. Comstock.

Wild Mammals of North America. Merriam. Holt.

ON INSECTS

A. B. C. of Bee Culture. Root. Root.

*Fieldbook of North American Insects. Lutz. Putnam.

The Insect Book. Howard. Doubleday, Doran.

The Moth Book. Holland. Doubleday, Doran.

Pocket Butterfly Guide. Holland. Doubleday, Doran.

(The many books by Henri Fabre on insects are recommended as fascinating reading, although not designed to aid in identifications.)

See also books under MISCELLANEOUS.

ON PLANTS

Bog-trotting for Orchids. Niles. Putnam.

*Fieldbook of American Wild Flowers. Matthews. Putnam.

*Fieldbook of Common Ferns. Durand. Putnam.

Fieldbook of Common Gilled Mushrooms. Thomas. Putnam.

How to Know the Ferns. Dana. Scribner's.

*How to Know the Wild Flowers. Dana. Scribner's.

*The Mushroom Book. Marshall. Doubleday, Doran.

Mushrooms. Atkinson. Holt.

*Mushrooms of Field and Wood. McKenny. John Day.

Nature's Garden. Blanchan. Doubleday, Doran.

Our Ferns and Their Haunts. Clute. Stokes.

Pocket Flower Guide. Reed. Reed.

On Trees and Shrubs

*Common Trees of New York. Illick. American Tree Assn.

*Familiar Trees and Their Leaves. Matthews. Appleton.

Fieldbook of American Trees and Shrubs. Matthews. Putnam.

Native Trees and How to Identify Them. Keeler. Scribner's.

North American Trees. Britton. Holt.

*The Tree Book. Rogers. Doubleday, Doran.

Trees in Winter. Blakeslee and Jarvis. Macmillan.

On Reptiles and Batrachians

Backyard Exploration. Howes. Doubleday, Doran.

Familiar Life of Field and Forest. Matthews. Appleton.

*The Frog Book. Dickerson. Doubleday, Doran.

*The Reptile Book. Ditmars. Doubleday, Doran.

On Fish and Aquariums

*American Food and Game Fishes. Jordan & Everman. Doubleday, Doran.

The Aquarium Book. Boulenger. Appleton.

*Fieldbook of Ponds and Streams. Morgan. Putnam.

*Fishes in the Home. Mellen. Dodd, Mead.

*Freshwater Aquarium and Its Contents. Eggeling and Ehrenberg. Holt.

Home Aquarium. Smith. Dutton.

Miscellaneous

Backyard Exploration. Howes. Doubleday, Doran.

*Book of Camping and Woodcraft. Kephart. Outing.

Book of Woodcraft. Seton. Doubleday, Doran.
*Fieldbook of Ponds and Streams. Morgan. Putnam.
Handbook of Nature Study. Comstock. Comstock.
Motor Camping. Long and Long. Dodd, Mead.
Romance of the Microscope. Ealand. Seeley.
Seeing Nature First. Weed. Lippincott.
Touring Afoot. Fordyce. Outing.
Walk, Look and Listen! Fuller. John Day.

There are many other good books. On the general subject of outdoor life and the mystery and charm of nature, an almost endless amount of enjoyment and information will be found in reading books by the following authors:

Ernest Thompson Seton
Henry Thoreau
John Burroughs
Gilbert White (Natural History of Selbourne)
John Muir
Earnest Ingersoll
L. H. Bailey
Walter Pritchard Eaton
T. Gilbert Pearson
Charles G. D. Roberts
Samuel Scoville, Jr.
Raymond Ditmars
W. L. Finley
A. A. Allen

Frank M. Chapman
William Beebe
Dallas Lore Sharp
Olive Thorne Miller
W. T. Hornaday
Bradford Torrey
Chester A. Reed
Herbert K. Job
Mabel Osgood Wright
Theodore Roosevelt
J. R. Sass
Ernest H. Baynes
William J. Long
Archibald Rutledge

THE

JOHN DAY

COMPANY
INC.

haps there we may become pioneers again! . . .
Salutamus Cæsar!

Yet, after all, why ascribe these changes, these
evolutions, these pioneer feelings, solely to New
England? Our land—all the world—is transforming under the incantations of steam and oil.
Wherever they sing in whirring wheels, humming
turbines, purring gears; keeping time to the
rhythmic beat of cylinders and throb of pistons;
backward retreats Nature, baulked and puzzled.
Is hers but a "strategic retirement to a stronger
position," or is it her defeat?

We cannot conceive of Nature defeated. "The
mechanical whirl-and-hurry world of the modern
city is illusory. All seem to hasten with it, accept
its tempo, speed with it down the ringing grooves
of industrialism. So in appearance, but not in reality. For the tempo of life is not life itself which it
hurries on through noise and change. The speedy,
the active ones seem to be the stream itself, but are
only its wavelets. Behind faces conformable to the
haste of modern experience are still philosophic
minds, contemplative, meditative, skeptical of
their own haste, brooding when they can. . . .
More daily is undertaken though not much more
worth counting is done. There is no better solu-

tion to the problem than Joshua's, who begged the sun to stand still while he finished his job at leisure; and, unlike him, we can expect no miracle. The busy world will go faster until it goes slower —though we shall not tarry here until the turn." *

Time is long and Nature has not been fleeting. The Egyptian-style in one great world era—four or five millenniums!—appeared to be the pattern of the universe; the *pax romanorum* seemed forever—longer than man's knowledge of the New World. (Someone has voiced his wonder at whether Cicero, standing at a corner of the Forum, could have dreamed of what twenty centuries have brought!) Our hands and thoughts may have changed, but our feelings are one with Ninevah and Tyre. Sunlight propels chlorophyl to feed the earth as it did in Sumeria; babies are yet born as Genghis Khan was born. Such fundamentals are an earnest of the future ahead of the race.

The triumph (!) of machines, the epoch of cities—shall men serve these two forever? This, in a last analysis, is the query which every nature-lover and peasant-heart refuses to answer: "Alas, yes!"

* From an editorial in the *Saturday Review of Literature*, April 6, 1929.

Part Four
BOOKS FOR IDENTIFICATIONS

Books for Identifications

(Those starred are the author's first choice)

ON BIRDS
American Ornithology. Reed. Reed.
Bird Neighbors. Blanchan. Doubleday, Doran.
Birds of America. (3 vols.) University Society.
Birds of the United States (East). Apgar. American
Book Co.
Birds That Hunt and Are Hunted. Blanchan. Dou-
bleday, Doran.
Book of Birds for Young People. Matthews. Putnam.
*Color Key to North American Birds. Chapman. Ap-
pleton.
Fieldbook of Wild Birds and Their Music. Matthews.
Putnam.
*Handbook of Birds of Eastern North America. Chap-
man. Appleton.
History of North American Birds. Ridgway, et al.
Little, Brown.
Key to North American Birds. Coues. Dana, Estes.
*Warblers of North America. Chapman. Appleton.

ON ANIMALS
*American Animals. Stone & Cram. Doubleday, Doran.
American Natural History. Hornaday. Scribner's.
Book of Animals. Nelson. National Geographical So-
ciety.

*Fieldbook of North American Mammals. Anthony. Putnam.
Life of Animals. Ingersoll. Macmillan.
The Pet Book. A. B. Comstock. Comstock.
Wild Mammals of North America. Merriam. Holt.

ON INSECTS
A. B. C. of Bee Culture. Root. Root.
*Fieldbook of North American Insects. Lutz. Putnam.
The Insect Book. Howard. Doubleday, Doran.
The Moth Book. Holland. Doubleday, Doran.
Pocket Butterfly Guide. Holland. Doubleday, Doran.
    (The many books by Henri Fabre on insects are recommended as fascinating reading, although not designed to aid in identifications.)
See also books under MISCELLANEOUS.

ON PLANTS
Bog-trotting for Orchids. Niles. Putnam.
*Fieldbook of American Wild Flowers. Matthews. Putnam.
*Fieldbook of Common Ferns. Durand. Putnam.
Fieldbook of Common Gilled Mushrooms. Thomas. Putnam.
How to Know the Ferns. Dana. Scribner's.
*How to Know the Wild Flowers. Dana. Scribner's.
*The Mushroom Book. Marshall. Doubleday, Doran.
Mushrooms. Atkinson. Holt.
*Mushrooms of Field and Wood. McKenny. John Day.
Nature's Garden. Blanchan. Doubleday, Doran.
Our Ferns and Their Haunts. Clute. Stokes.
Pocket Flower Guide. Reed. Reed.

On Trees and Shrubs

  *Common Trees of New York. Illick. American Tree
    Assn.
  *Familiar Trees and Their Leaves. Matthews. Apple-
    ton.
  Fieldbook of American Trees and Shrubs. Matthews.
    Putnam.
  Native Trees and How to Identify Them. Keeler.
    Scribner's.
  North American Trees. Britton. Holt.
  *The Tree Book. Rogers. Doubleday, Doran.
  Trees in Winter. Blakeslee and Jarvis. Macmillan.

On Reptiles and Batrachians

  Backyard Exploration. Howes. Doubleday, Doran.
  Familiar Life of Field and Forest. Matthews. Apple-
    ton.
  *The Frog Book. Dickerson. Doubleday, Doran.
  *The Reptile Book. Ditmars. Doubleday, Doran.

On Fish and Aquariums

  *American Food and Game Fishes. Jordan & Everman.
    Doubleday, Doran.
  The Aquarium Book. Boulenger. Appleton.
  *Fieldbook of Ponds and Streams. Morgan. Putnam.
  *Fishes in the Home. Mellen. Dodd, Mead.
  *Freshwater Aquarium and Its Contents. Eggeling and
    Ehrenberg. Holt.
  Home Aquarium. Smith. Dutton.

Miscellaneous

  Backyard Exploration. Howes. Doubleday, Doran.
  *Book of Camping and Woodcraft. Kephart. Outing.

Book of Woodcraft. Seton. Doubleday, Doran.
*Fieldbook of Ponds and Streams. Morgan. Putnam.
Handbook of Nature Study. Comstock. Comstock.
Motor Camping. Long and Long. Dodd, Mead.
Romance of the Microscope. Ealand. Seeley.
Seeing Nature First. Weed. Lippincott.
Touring Afoot. Fordyce. Outing.
Walk, Look and Listen! Fuller. John Day.

There are many other good books. On the general subject of outdoor life and the mystery and charm of nature, an almost endless amount of enjoyment and information will be found in reading books by the following authors:

Ernest Thompson Seton
Henry Thoreau
John Burroughs
Gilbert White (Natural History of Selbourne)
John Muir
Earnest Ingersoll
L. H. Bailey
Walter Pritchard Eaton
T. Gilbert Pearson
Charles G. D. Roberts
Samuel Scoville, Jr.
Raymond Ditmars
W. L. Finley
A. A. Allen

Frank M. Chapman
William Beebe
Dallas Lore Sharp
Olive Thorne Miller
W. T. Hornaday
Bradford Torrey
Chester A. Reed
Herbert K. Job
Mabel Osgood Wright
Theodore Roosevelt
J. R. Sass
Ernest H. Baynes
William J. Long
Archibald Rutledge

THE

JOHN DAY

COMPANY

INC.